南無本師釋迦牟尼佛

NAMO FUNDAMENTAL TEACHER SHAKYAMUNI BUDDHA

在我的世界裏，

眾生都是由蓮華化生，故身體清淨無染。

因為阿彌陀佛發這種大願，

所以一切眾生都應該修念佛法門。

"In my land,

all living beings are born transformationally from lotus flowers,

so their bodies will be pure and have no defilement."

Because of these great vows made by Amitabha Buddha,

all living beings should cultivate

the Dharma-door of reciting the Buddha's name.

平時要學著念佛，修淨土法門，
等到臨命終時才不會驚慌失措，
而得以平安往生極樂世界。

It's important to practice reciting the Buddha's name
and cultivate the Pure Land Dharma-door on a regular basis.
Then you won't panic at the time of death,
and you'll be able to attain peaceful rebirth
in the Land of Ultimate Bliss.

佛經是釋迦牟尼佛金口所說，
一字不能改，一字不能漏，
否則不但無功，反而有過。

The Sutras were personally spoken by Shakyamuni Buddha.
Not a word can be changed, and not a word can be omitted.
Otherwise, there will be no merit but only offenses.

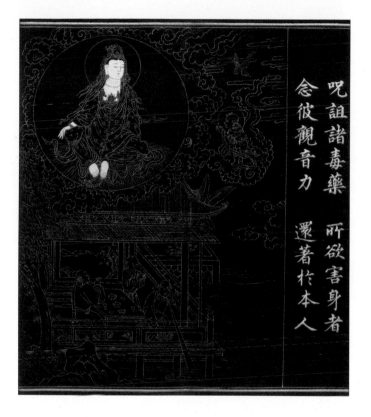

呪詛諸毒藥　所欲害身者
念彼觀音力　還著於本人

講經說法、印經流通、翻譯經典、繪畫佛像，
這都是修慧的法門。

Speaking Dharma, printing and circulating Sutras,
translating Sutras, making Buddha images—
These are ways of cultivating wisdom.

阿羅漢。諸漏已盡。無復煩惱。

逮得己利。盡諸有結。心得自在。

The Arhats had exhausted all outflows

and had no further afflictions.

Having attained self-benefit,

they had exhausted the bonds of all existence

and their minds had attained self-mastery.

地藏王菩薩的願力最大，他説：
「地獄未空，誓不成佛；
眾生度盡，方證菩提。」
Earth Store Bodhisattva has the greatest vows. He has said,
"As long as the hells are not empty, I will not become a Buddha.
Only when all living beings have been completely liberated
will I become a Buddha."

我們做人，一定要本著
「孝、悌、忠、信、禮、義、廉、恥」八德為標準。

In being a person,we should take the eight virtues—
filial piety,brotherhood, loyalty, trustworthiness,
propriety, righteousness, incorruptibility,
and a sense of shame—as our standard.

善事做多了，善功德具足了，
就生到天上，享受天上的快樂。
但這不究竟，等到天福享盡時，
仍然墮落在輪迴中，接受應受的果報。
If we do many good deeds
and achieve wholesome merit and virtue,
we can be reborn in the heavens to enjoy celestial happiness.
However, the state of celestial beings is not an ultimate one.
when they exhaust their celestial blessings,
They must re-enter the transmigratory cycle
to receive the retribution they deserve.

世間的一切，都是成住壞空，循環無端，
若能明白這種道理，對於世界一切的一切，
都不要執著，都不要有煩惱，
能看破放下，就一切都沒有問題了。

Everything in the world goes through the stages

of coming into being, dwelling, destruction, and emptiness.

There is no beginning to the cycle.

If you understand this,

you should not cherish attachments to anything.

Don't let anything vex you.

「龍」究竟是什麼樣子？
一般人是不知道的。
除非開五眼的聖人才知道龍的真面目。
What do dragons look like?
Ordinary people don't know.
Only sages who have opened the five eyes
know what dragons really look like.

凡是出家修行，一心求道，
什麼也不要，什麼也不貪。
就是一棵芥草，也不能隨便送給人，
也不能隨便向人索取。

People who have entered the monastic life to cultivate
should seek the Way single-mindedly,
wanting nothing else and being greedy for nothing.
You can't carelessly give even a mustard seed to other people,
nor can you ask people for one.

梵語禪那波羅蜜，此云靜慮細進參；
山高水深無所畏，始知天外別有天。

The Sanskrit words dhyana paramita

Mean to contemplate in stillness

And subtly advance your investigation.

Have no fear of high mountains or deep waters;

Then you will discover the sky beyond the sky.

下棋，總有輸贏，

下棋的人，永遠不是輸，永遠不是贏。

這種哲理，令我們對境明心，因事悟道。

In chess, there are always winners and losers.

A chess player won't always lose, nor will he always win.

With that principle, we can understand our mind

and awaken to the Way as we face situations.

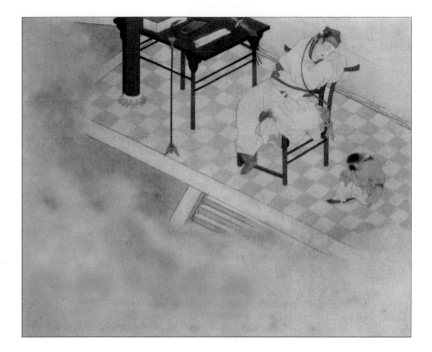

人來到這個世界，

把真的放下，拿起假的，

所以生生世世背覺合塵，醉生夢死。

When people come into this world,

they put down the real and pick up the unreal.

That is why in life after life we turn against enlightenment,

unite with the dust, and muddle our way through life

as if drunk or in a dream.

宣化上人德相

The Venerable Master Hsuan Hua

宣化上人開示錄

（八）

Venerable Master Hua's
Talks on Dharma

Volume Eight

宣化上人開示錄

（八）

佛經翻譯委員會
英　譯

法界佛教總會
佛經翻譯委員會
法界佛教大學
出　版

Venerable Master Hua's
Talks on Dharma

Volume Eight

English translation by the
Buddhist Text Translation Society

Buddhist Text Translation Society
Dharma Realm Buddhist University
Dharma Realm Buddhist Association
Burlingame, California U.S.A.

宣化上人開示錄（八）
Venerable Master Hua's Talks on Dharma
Volume Eight

Published and translated by:
    Buddhist Text Translation Society
    1777 Murchison Drive,
    Burlingame, CA 94010-4504

First Chinese edition published 1984,
Dharma Realm Buddhist Books Distribution Society, as
宣化上人開示錄（五）
(hsüan hua shang ren kai shi lu—wu)

First bilingual edition 2001
(Fifth Chinese edition, First English edition)
04 03 02 01   10 9 8 7 6 5 4 3 2 1

ISBN 0-88139-855-1
Library of Congress Catalog Card Number: 96-136258

Printed in Taiwan

Note: Pinyin is used for the romanization of Chinese words,
       except for proper names which retain familiar romanizations.

佛經翻譯委員會八項基本守則
The Eight Guidelines of
The Buddhist Text Translation Society

1. 從事翻譯工作者不得抱有個人的名利。
   A volunteer must free him/herself from the motives of personal
   fame and profit.

2. 從事翻譯工作者不得貢高我慢，必須以虔誠恭敬的
   態度來工作。
   A volunteer must cultivate a respectful and sincere attitude free
   from arrogance and conceit.

3. 從事翻譯工作者不得自讚毀他。
   A volunteer must refrain from aggrandizing his/her work and
   denigrating that of others.

4. 從事翻譯工作者不得自以為是，對他人作品吹毛求疵。
   A volunteer must not establish him/herself as the standard of
   correctness and suppress the work of others with his or her
   fault-finding.

5. 從事翻譯工作者必須以佛心為己心。
   A volunteer must take the Buddha-mind as his/her own mind.

6. 從事翻譯工作者必須運用擇法眼來辨別正確的道理。
   A volunteer must use the wisdom of Dharma-Selecting Vision
   to determine true principles.

7. 從事翻譯工作者必須懇請十方大德長老來印證其翻譯。
   A volunteer must request Virtuous Elders in the ten directions
   to certify his/her translations.

8. 從事翻譯工作者之作品在獲得印證之後，必須努力弘揚流通
   經、律、論以及佛書以光大佛教。
   A volunteer must endeavor to propagate the teachings by printing
   Sutras, Shastra texts, and Vinaya texts when the translations are
   certified as being correct.

目　錄

CONTENTS

至誠孝順感天地

為了使母親病癒，
他發願要剁手供養佛。

在東北哈爾濱南邊，有個村莊，名叫大南溝屯，這
個地方有位孝子，姓高，名叫德福。他母親患重病
，中西醫都束手無策，爲了使母親病癒，他發願要
剁手供養佛。這番孝心，感動天地，將他的母親從
死魔中奪回生命。這件事曾經轟動一時，老少婦孺
皆知高德福是一位大孝子。這個公案經過如下：

他母親患重病，粒米不食，滴水不飲，奄奄一息，
命在旦夕。於是他到三緣寺（這天是浴佛節，正舉
行大法會，參加的善信約有數百人），在佛前上香
，三拜之後，拿出菜刀正要剁左手的時候，被人發

2

Exceptional Filiality Moves Heaven and Earth

In order to save his mother he vowed to cut off his hand and offer it to the Buddha.

In Manchuria, south of the city of Harbin, in the village Da-nan-gou there lived a filial son called Defu Gao. His mother was sick and none of the Chinese or Western doctors could cure her. In order to save his mother he vowed to cut off his hand and offer it to the Buddha. His filial act moved heaven and earth, and his mother was rescued from the clutches of death. This event caused quite a stir at the time. Even women and children knew that Gao was a greatly filial son. The story goes like this:

Gao's mother was very ill. She could neither eat or drink, and she was dying. Gao went to Three Conditions Monastery (it happened to be Shakyamuni Buddha's birthday, so there was a big Dharma assembly going on, with a few hundred Buddhists attending) and lit a stick of incense in

現了，即時制止他，有人就問他：「為什麼要剁手呢？」他說：「為了母親的病，所以發心剁手供養佛。」當時有位居士，名叫李景華，對他說：「你快到方丈室去，求方丈和尚，他有神通，可能可以救你母親。」

他到方丈室，見到方丈和尚，說明來意，方丈和尚對他說：「你去求安慈法師，他有辦法，能治好你母親的病。」他又來到我寮房，請我慈悲，給他母親治病。我聽說他是個孝子，於是乎就答應了，對他說：「你騎自行車先回家，我隨後就到。」他很高興走了。可是他騎自行車必走大路，我從小路走，比他先到十分鐘。

他一進門，看見我已坐在炕上，就很驚訝地說：「師父！您怎麼比我先到？我騎自行車，卻沒有您走得快！」這時，全家大小都來叩頭，這就是「平時不燒香，臨時抱佛腳。」於是我寫了一道疏文，令他母親的病一定要好，等疏文焚化之後，病人就安詳地睡著了，大家也都休息了。

front of the Buddha. After three bows, he took out a kitchen knife and was just about to chop off his left hand, when he was discovered and stopped by some people. When asked why he wanted to cut off his hand, he explained that he'd vowed to chop off his hand and offer it to the Buddha because of his mother's illness. At that time a layperson called Jinghua Li said to him, "Go to the Abbot's office and plead with him. He has spiritual powers. Maybe he can save your mother."

Gao went to the Abbot's office and explained why he had come. The Abbot told him, "Why don't you go ask Dharma Master An Ci. He can cure your mother's illness." So he came to my room asking me to be compassionate and attend to his mother's illness. I had heard he was a filial son, so I promised to help him. I said to him, "Ride your bike home first. I'll be there right away." He left happily. Since he was riding a bike, he had to go by the main road, while I took a shortcut. I arrived there ten minutes before him.

When he came in the door and saw me sitting on the brick bed, he was shocked and said, "Master, how did you get here before me? You walked faster than I rode the bike!" Then the whole family came to bow to me. This was a typical case of people who usually never lit incense, but were seeking help from the Buddha in an emergency. I wrote a declaration vowing that his mother would get well. After the declaration was burned, the mother fell asleep peacefully. Everyone went to bed.

第二天早晨，病人就坐起來了，喚他兒子的乳名，「舉子！舉子！我很餓，我想吃點粥。」高德福聽到母親能講話，高興得無法形容，急忙爲母親煮粥，病人吃了一碗粥，就恢復說話的能力。（她有八天不言不語，不飲不食，唇也焦，舌也黑了。）

高德福問他母親：「媽！您老人家這幾天覺得怎麼樣啊？」

他母親說：「啊！我走丟了，找不到回家的路，沒有日頭，沒有月亮，也沒有星辰，一片烏黑，不知東南西北方向，在黑暗中摸索了好幾天。昨天晚上，有個和尚他把我送回來了！」高德福一聽，心裏明白，又問：「媽！是什麼樣子的出家人？」他母親說：「那位和尚穿很破的衣服。」高德福用手指著我，問：「媽！您老人家看看，是不是那位和尚？」老太太仔細地看，她說：「就是他送我回家的！」這時，全家就都來皈依我，而老太太的病也慢慢好了。

一九八三年七月十五日開示

6

The next morning, the mother sat up and called her son by his nickname, "Juzi, Juzi! I'm hungry. I'd like some rice porridge." When the boy realized that his mother could talk, he felt unspeakable joy. Quickly he cooked some porridge for her. She ate a bowl of porridge and regained enough strength to talk. (For eight days she hadn't been able to talk, eat or drink. Her lips were parched and her tongue had turned black.)

"Mother, how did you feel during the past few days?" the boy asked.

"Oh! I got lost, and I couldn't find my way back home. It was dark. There were no stars, moon, or sun. I groped in the dark for days and didn't know which way to turn. Last night, a monk brought me home." When the boy heard that, he understood.

"Mother, what did this monk look like?"

The mother said, "He was dressed in rag robes."

"Mother, look, was he the monk?" the boy asked, pointing to me. The old woman looked at me carefully, and said, "That's the one who took me home!" The whole family then took refuge with me, and the old woman gradually got well.

A talk given on July 15, 1983

果舜焚身供佛

身體雖然成為黑炭，
但是其心完整，未被火化。

我在東北的時候，收了一個弟子，法名果舜。他俗姓姚，一般人叫他老姚，他家住在哈爾濱南二十里大南溝屯。他在未皈依三寶之前，是一個遊手好閒的浪子，不但吸鴉片，而且還打嗎啡，可以說是吃喝嫖賭，無所不為。

當時日本統治東北，成立滿洲國，利用清朝廢帝宣統，做滿洲國的皇帝，成為日本的傀儡，一切的政權操縱在日本人手中。日本為了防止蘇聯的侵略，於是在黑河一帶建築國防工程，到處抓勞工去服役，只有貢獻，沒有酬勞。凡是進到勞工營的人，只

8

How Guo Shun Burned His Body as an Offering to the Buddha

Although Guo Shun's body had been burned black, his heart was still intact and unburnt.

When I was in Manchuria, I accepted a disciple and gave him the Dharma name Guo Shun. His surname was Yao, and people called him Old Yao. He lived about twenty miles south of Harbin in Da-nan-gou Village. Before he took refuge with the Triple Jewel, he was a loafer who smoked opium and shot himself up with morphine. As to eating, drinking, playing with women, and gambling, he did all of that and more.

Manchuria was under the rule of the Japanese at that time. They founded the state of Manchukuo and set up the dethroned Qin dynasty emperor, Xuantong as the puppet emperor. The Japanese held all the political power. They conscripted laborers everywhere for their defense construction projects in the Black River area, which were aimed at

有終日憂愁，不知何年才能回到溫暖的家鄉。談起勞工營的生活，就令人不寒而慄，那簡直是人間地獄，苦不堪言。

果舜當時是無業遊民，就被日本兵抓去，送到黑河勞工營。在那裏白天做牛馬的工作，夜間蓋草包睡覺，不能禦寒，他時時在想：「怎樣能逃出勞工營呢？」因為勞工營的四周，設有強力的電網，如果有任何眾生撞上，馬上會被電觸死。雖然有電網的威脅，可是他受不了慘無人道的虐待，時時總想找機會逃走。

有一天晚上，他為了投奔自由，不顧生命的安全，決定離開人間地獄的勞工營。於是他利用到廁所的機會，想逃出勞工營，正要啟步逃走之時，忽然來了一位白鬍鬚的老人，對他說：「現在不是你逃走的時候，因為你的苦還沒有受完，你再忍耐一段時間，等到脫苦的時候，我再通知你。希望你提高警覺，不可錯過機會。」老人說完之後，就不知去向了。果舜相信老人的話，就返回營房。

大約兩個禮拜之後，果舜在夢中遇到白鬍鬚的老人

preventing the Soviet Union from invading. The laborers were forced to work without pay, and they never knew when they would be able to return to their hometowns. The labor camps were hell on earth; the suffering was beyond words. It made people shiver just to speak of their experience there.

Guo Shun had been a loafer when he was taken to the Black River labor camp by the Japanese soldiers. During the day he was forced to toil like an ox, and at night he slept in a bale of grass which did not protect him from the cold. He constantly tried to find ways to escape. The camp was surrounded by a high-voltage electric fence which would electrify anything that touched it. Unable to take the cruel treatment, he constantly sought for a chance to escape, notwithstanding the electric barrier.

One night, desperate to leave that hell-like camp and regain his freedom, Guo Shun decided to attempt an escape when he went to the toilet. When he was just about ready to take off, an old man with a silvery beard suddenly came by and said, "This is not the time for you to escape. Your suffering has not been finished. Be patient. When the time comes, I will let you know. I hope you'll be alert and not let the chance slip by." After saying that, the old man vanished. Guo Shun believed him and returned to the camp.

About two weeks later, Guo Shun dreamed of the old man with the silvery beard, who said, "Today you should es-

，對他這樣説：「今天是你逃走的時候，在門外有隻白狗，你跟著牠走，萬無一失。切記！切記！」他驚喜而醒，來到門外，果然有隻白狗，在那兒等著他。果舜聽老人的指示，白狗在前邊走，他在後邊跟著，走到電網處，白狗一躍，跳過電網，這是示範動作，令果舜照樣學習。果舜這個時候，福至心靈，生出靈感來，將遮寒的草包放在電網的上邊，然後一躍而過，就這樣平安無事逃出虎口。等他再回頭，白狗卻不見了，大概這是神人的幫助。

他爲避日本兵的追捕，白天藏在樹林中，渴時就飲溪水，餓時就吃些草葉，夜間才敢行路。這樣經過多日的辛苦，才回到家鄉。受了這次打擊之後，他覺得人生是苦，就決定出家修道。他到處找廟，都不肯收容他，當他來到三緣寺時，因爲所穿的衣服破爛不堪，別人認爲他是乞丐，爲生活而出家，所以也不肯收留他。

他正在大廟不收，小廟不留的時候，不知從什麼地方來了一個怪人，好像討飯的乞丐一樣。這個人自我介紹，説他是老修行，會三十六天罡，七十二地

cape. There will be a white dog outside the door. Just follow it and you'll be all right. Remember what I've told you." Guo Shun woke up with joy. When he went to the door, there really was a white dog waiting for him. Guo Shun followed the old man's instructions and followed right behind the dog. When they reached the electric fence, the white dog jumped over it. Guo Shun knew he was supposed to follow suit. In a sudden inspiration, he took a bale of grass, put it over the fence, and then jumped over it. He was safe. When he turned around, the white dog was gone. Perhaps it had been a heavenly being coming to his aid.

In order to elude the Japanese soldiers who were searching for him, he hid in the woods by day, drinking from the streams and eating grass or leaves to satisfy his hunger. He dared to walk only at night. After many days of arduous travel, he arrived in his hometown. After his experience in the labor camp, he felt that life was full of suffering, and so he decided to become a monk and practice the spiritual path. He went to all the temples, but none would take him in. When he went to Three Conditions Monastery, people would not accept him there either because they thought he was a beggar (from his ragged clothes) who wanted to become a monk just so he could get food and shelter.

When he had been turned down by all temples large and small, Guo Shun met a strange man who looked like a beggar. No one knew where he was from, but he introduced himself as an old cultivator capable of all sorts of magical

煞的法術，能騰空駕雲，呼風喚雨，能醫治一切疑難雜症，有妙手回春的神技。這個人自吹自擂，鬼話連篇，胡謅亂說一陣，沒有人相信，只有果舜相信，就拜他為師，用不正當手段得來的錢，供養他的生活。日子久了，果舜發現他沒有真本事，也是個無賴漢，於是離他而去。

有一天，我到大南溝屯去，給高德福的母親治病。她患重病，中西醫都束手無策，我用神咒給她加持，結果不藥而癒。全屯知道這個消息，都認為是神蹟。老姚（果舜）知道了，就來到我面前，長跪不起，要求跟我出家，我當時不理他，面壁而坐，約有一個小時之久。我回頭一看，老姚仍然跪在地上，我問他：「你在做什麼？」

老姚說：「請師父慈悲，收我為徒弟。」

我說：「你想跟我出家嗎？可是我沒有什麼德行，也沒有什麼功夫可以教導你，會令你失望的。」他說：「只要收我為徒弟，我就心滿意足，別無所求。」

arts. He claimed he could fly in the sky, ride the clouds, call the wind and rain, and cure any disease, even bringing the dead back to life. No one except Guo Shun believed his nonsense and lies. Guo Shun bowed to him as his teacher and offered to support him with money which he had obtained by improper means. After a while, he discovered that the man was a scoundrel with no skills at all, and so he left him.

One day I went to Da-nan-gou Village to treat Defu Gao's sick mother, whom none of the Chinese or Western doctors had been able to cure. I used no medicine to cure her, but simply the power of a mantra. The villagers thought it was a miracle. When Old Yao (Guo Shun) heard about it, he came and knelt before me, asking permission to enter the monastic life. I paid no attention to him and just sat in meditation facing the wall for about an hour. When I turned around and saw that he was still kneeling there, I asked him, "What are you doing?"

"Teacher, please be compassionate and accept me as your disciple."

"You want me to let you enter the monastic life?" I asked. "I don't have any virtue, and I have no skills to teach you. You will be disappointed."

"I will be content as long as you take me as your disciple. I have no other wish," he replied.

15

我說：「出家是苦事，要忍人所不能忍的事，要讓人所不能讓的事，要吃人所不能吃的苦，要受人所不能受的氣，你能嗎？如果能的話，我就收你爲徒弟；要是不能，不要跟著我出家。」

老姚不加考慮，即時就說：「一切苦我都能忍受，出家雖然苦，我相信也沒有勞工營苦。我有信心，能受得了。」

經過這番的問答，我認爲他能受得苦，於是帶他回到三緣寺，出家爲沙彌，令他擔任廚房的工作。他做事很謹慎，修行很用功，可是師兄弟與他無緣，時常欺負他，他實在忍無可忍之下，向我訴苦：「師父！師兄弟無緣無故罵我，我怎麼辦呢？」

我說：「你既然受不了，可以單獨修行。」他就到大南溝屯的西山龍王廟旁邊一塊空地，自己搭了一間茅棚，做爲修行的道場。

落成當天，佛像開光，果舜來三緣寺請我去開光，我帶領幾個弟子，一同前去。當天晚間，來了十條

"The life of a monk is very bitter. You have to endure what other people cannot endure, yield where others cannot yield, undergo bitterness that others cannot undergo, and bear abuses that other people cannot bear. Can you do that? If you can, I will accept you as my disciple. Otherwise, do not ask to enter the monastic life."

Old Yao replied without hesitation, "I can take any kind of suffering. Monastic life may be bitter, but I doubt it's as bitter as working in a labor camp. I am confident that I can bear it."

Hearing him say that, I believed he could take the suffering, and so I took him back to Three Conditions Monastery. He renounced the life of a householder and worked in the kitchen as a novice monk. He was a careful worker and a diligent cultivator. However, he had no affinities with the other monks, and was often bullied by them. When he could take it no more, he came to me and asked, "Teacher, my Dharma brothers are always scolding me for no reason at all. What can I do?"

"If you cannot take it, you may cultivate alone," I told him. Then he went to Dragon King Temple, in the hills west of the village, and built a hut on the vacant lot next to the temple.

When he completed the hut, he came to Three Conditions Monastery to invite me to bless the Buddha image. I took a

龍（化人身），要求皈依三寶。這時初夏時節，天旱無雨，禾苗枯黃，靠天吃飯的農人，垂頭喪氣嘆命苦，有時無語問蒼天，祈禱老天爺：「可憐吧！慈悲吧！降點甘露吧！」我對眾龍説：「你們的工作是行雨，天這樣乾旱，為什麼不降雨呢？」

諸龍説：「沒有玉皇大帝的命令，不敢降雨，否則要受處罰。」

我説：「你們到玉皇大帝的凌霄寶殿去，請大帝慈悲，在此處四周四十里以內降雨。明天降雨，後天授皈依，這是我們交換的條件。」

第二天，果然在四十里以內，降甘露雨，禾苗得到雨水的滋潤，都欣欣向榮，到秋天收穫時，五穀豐收比往年更多。第三天，諸龍來茅棚佛堂前，受三皈依。為了紀念這件事，就把這個茅棚，命名為「龍雨茅棚」，特書匾額，懸在茅棚上。

後來果舜發願焚身供養佛，他自備木柴和汽油，然後坐在柴上，自燃汽油，將身焚化成灰。次日，村

few disciples along with me. That night ten dragons (manifesting in human form) came and requested to take refuge with the Triple Jewel. It was early summer, and there was a drought. The grain sprouts were parched, and the farmers were in very low spirits, for they depended on the rain. Sometimes they silently prayed to Heaven for rain. I told the dragons, "It's your job to make the rain fall. Why has it been so dry? Why don't you let it rain?"

"We dare not make the rain fall if the Jade Emperor hasn't given us the order. If we did, we'd be punished."

"Well, you go to the Jade Emperor and ask him to be compassionate and allow rain to fall within a fourteen mile radius of this place. I'll transmit the Three Refuges to you the day after you make it rain. Those are my conditions."

The next day, it really rained within a fourteen mile radius. The young grain shoots sprang to life, and that fall, there was an abundant harvest of all the crops, much better than in previous years. The day after the rain, the dragons came to the hut and received the Three Refuges. I named the hut "Dragon Rain Cottage" in memory of this event. I wrote those words on a plaque and hung it on the gate.

Later on, Guo Shun vowed to burn his body as an offering to the Buddha. He gathered a pile of firewood, doused it with gasoline, and seated himself on top of it. Then he lit a fire and burned himself to ashes. The next day, the villagers

19

人發現「龍雨茅棚」被大火所燒燬，前來觀看，才見果舜的身體雖然成爲黑炭，但是其心完整，未被火化。大家嘆息不已，於是將果舜的骨灰及心，埋葬在此處。

世間的一切，都是成住壞空，循環無端，若能明白這種道理，對於世界一切的一切，都不要執著，都不要有煩惱，能看破放下，就一切都沒有問題了。

saw that Dragon Rain Cottage had been burned and went to see what had happened. Although Guo Shun's body had been burned black, his heart was still intact and unburnt. Everyone was amazed, and they buried Guo Shun's ashes and his heart there.

Everything in the world goes through the stages of coming into being, dwelling, destruction, and emptiness. There is no beginning to the cycle. If you understand this, you should not cherish attachments to anything. Don't let anything vex you. If you can understand and let go of everything, there will be no problems.

果能出家的因緣

他有知過必改的勇氣，
希望你們也能知過能改。

有一年的冬天，我到哈爾濱南邊上號的地方去辦事，經過某個旅店，這個旅店的老闆是我的皈依弟子，所以我就進去看他。他對我說：「師父！我的店中住了一個吃素的人，他想出家修行，可是找不到廟。師父您能不能收他為徒弟？」

我說：「他為什麼要出家？」

老闆說：「他是山東人，以裁縫為業，和一個抽大菸（鴉片菸）的女人同居。有一天，他不在家，這個女人將他所儲蓄的錢，全部拿走了，晚上等到裁縫回家時，才發現自己人財兩空。他受了這個打擊

22

How Guo Neng Entered the Monastic Life

He had the courage to correct his mistakes when he recognized he was wrong. I hope you can also correct your mistakes when you become aware of them.

One winter, I went to a place south of Harbin to take care of some business. On my way, I passed a hotel owned by my disciple, and I went in to say hello. The owner said, "Dharma Master, there's a person staying in my hotel who wants to become a monk, but he can't find a temple. He's a vegetarian. Could you accept him as your disciple?"

"Why does he want to become a monk?" I asked.

"He's a tailor from Shandong province, and he lived with a woman who smoked opium. One day when he was out, the woman made off with all his savings. When he came home to find the woman and all his money gone, he felt that life is totally meaningless. And so he has decided to renounce the

，就感到心灰意冷，覺得人生無趣，所以決定出家修行。他到哈爾濱南岡極樂寺，想跟如光法師出家，可是如光法師不收他爲徒弟，他無奈住在我的店裏，天天愁眉不展，悶悶不樂，不和任何人說話，實在很可憐！」

我說：「把他叫來！」老闆去叫他，但他不來，大概他看我穿著破袍，不像個有廟的和尚。第二次叫他來，他勉強來了，開口便說：「你叫我來做什麼？」（山東人心直口快）

我對他說：「我來這裏，就是找你。」他很驚奇地問：「你認識我嗎？」

我說：「現在不談這些，你願意出家嗎？我的廟上缺個做飯的人，你可以藉此修苦行，有飯給你吃，有屋給你住，可是沒有錢給你花，你願意去嗎？」

他聽我說可以收他做徒弟，很高興地說：「我願意去！」隨即跟著我去廟上，擔任做飯的工作，於是受沙彌戒，法名叫果能。

life of a householder and cultivate. He went to Ultimate Bliss Monastery south of Harbin and asked to join the monastic order under Dharma Master Ru Guang, but he was turned down. Not knowing what to do, he came to my hotel. He is very unhappy and doesn't talk to anyone. It's a real pity."

"Go get him!" I said. The owner went to call him, but he wouldn't come out. Maybe he saw my rag robes and thought I didn't look like a monk who had a temple. After being called a second time, he came reluctantly. The first thing he said was, "What do you want from me?" (Shandong people are very frank and outspoken.)

"I came to get you," I said.

"Do you know me?" he asked in surprise.

"Let's not talk about that. Do you want to become a monk? My temple needs a cook. You can take this chance to cultivate ascetic practices. You'll be fed and have a place to stay, but no cash. Are you willing to come?"

Hearing that I was going to take him as my disciple, he replied happily, "I'll come!" He returned to the temple with me, worked as a cook, took the novice precepts, and received the Dharma name Guo Neng.

有一天，他心血來潮，在一間小屋造了一個炕，但是事先沒有經過廟上的人同意，他就自作主張。當時，我不知内情，可是就有人在我面前說風涼話，說：「收徒弟，自己管不了徒弟，眞丟人！徒弟沒有做完，就當起祖師來了！」我覺得奇怪，於是到後邊看看，究竟發生什麼事情？遇見一位師兄弟，他對我說：「你的徒弟造反了，不守道場規矩，沒有經過同意，就私自造火炕。」

我進他房間一看，果然他坐在炕上打坐，他見我進來，下炕頂禮，我問他：「這炕是誰教你造的？」他說：「沒有人。」我說：「既然沒有人教你造，你怎麼可以自己隨隨便便就造炕，這是犯規矩的！」他無話可說，就跪在地上，我說：「你在佛前懺悔，跪一炷香。」

我走了之後，他沒有到佛前跪香，又回到炕上補衣服。半小時之後，我到佛堂去，不見他在跪香。我又到他房間去，問他：「果能，你爲什麼不跪香？」他說：「等一會兒。」

One day, on a sudden impulse, he made a brick bed in his small room. He did this without asking for permission from the people in charge of the temple. I was not aware of it either. But then some people sarcastically commented, "You take a disciple, but you can't even discipline him. What a disgrace Your disciple thinks he's already a patriarch!"

Thinking this strange, I went to the back of the temple to see what on earth had happened. On the way, I met a Dharma brother who said, "Your disciple has revolted. He's built a brick bed for himself and broken the rules of the Way-place."

I went into Guo Neng's room and found him sitting on the brick bed meditating. When he saw me, he came down from the bed and bowed to me.

I asked him, "Who told you to make this brick bed?" He answered, "No one." I said, "If no one told you to make it, how could you go ahead and construct it on your own? That's against the rules!" He had nothing to say, he just kept kneeling. I said, "Go and repent in front of the Buddha. Kneel for the time it takes for one stick of incense to burn down [about an hour]."

But after I left, he did not go to kneel in front of the Buddha. He went back to the bed to mend his clothes. Half an hour later, I went to the Buddha Hall and didn't see him there. I returned to his room and asked him, "Guo Neng! Why didn't you kneel?" He said, "Later."

我說：「你不願意跪香，我替你跪香。」於是我到佛前上香，跪在磚地上。

他看我跪著，無可奈何在我後邊哀求地說：「師父！我知道錯了，請您原諒！請您起來，我現在跪著呢！」我說：「我管不了徒弟，可是我能管得了自己。」經過這次的教訓，以後他處處守規矩，時時用功修行，他有知過必改的勇氣，希望你們也能知過能改。

"If you're not willing to kneel for one incense, I'll do it for you." I went to the Buddha Hall, lit a stick of incense, and knelt down on the brick floor.

He saw me kneeling and begged me to stop, saying, "Master! I know I was wrong. Please forgive me. Please get up! I'm kneeling now!" I said, "I can't discipline my disciple, but I can discipline myself." After this incident he always followed the rules and cultivated diligently at all times. He had the courage to correct his mistakes when he recognized he was wrong. I hope you can also correct your mistakes when you become aware of them.

用智慧管理大眾飲食

沒有飯吃的人，
都是因為在往昔糟蹋食物。

有人問我：「這次慶祝觀世音菩薩成道法會，會有
多少善信參加？」我說：「也許有三、四個人吧！
」今天我統計來參加法會的人，大約有四百多人，
這人又問我：「是不是一個人當做百人？」我說：
「我不懂。」

今年觀音法會，大眾比往年誠心，往年法會在吃飯
的時候，大家都高談闊論，不守齋堂的規矩；吃完
飯，在碗中剩下很多菜飯，丟到垃圾桶內，或者吃
完飯後，也不隨喜功德就走了。今年的情形大有改
善，不但不講話，也不糟蹋食物，很少人趕著回三

Wisely Manage the
Food Resources of the Temple

**People who have nothing to eat now
wasted food in past lives.**

Somebody asked me how many Buddhists would attend this celebration of Guanyin Bodhisattva's Accomplishment of the Way. I said, "Well, maybe three or four!" Today I counted about four hundred people in attendance. The same person asked me again, "Did you take a hundred for one?" I said, "I don't understand."

This year, people who attended the Guanyin Dharma assembly were more sincere than in previous years. In the earlier Dharma assemblies, people talked during meals and didn't follow the rules of the dining hall. A lot of leftover food was thrown into the garbage, and people left after the meal without finishing the Dharma assembly. This year the situation has improved a lot. Not only was there no talking during meals, but food was not wasted, and very few

藩市，這是很可喜的事。

以後再有法會時應該提醒大家：「吃飯時不要講話，飯後不要糟蹋東西，要愛惜食物。」有古詩云：

> 鋤禾日當午，
> 汗滴禾下土；
> 誰知盤中餐，
> 粒粒皆辛苦。

一般人不知道粒粒皆辛苦的道理，所以任意暴殄天物，隨便糟蹋食物。要知道世上沒有飯吃的人，都是因為在往昔糟蹋食物，所以今生才受沒有飯吃的果報。這個淺顯的道理，必須告訴大家，讓大家明白之後，才不會糟蹋東西。

管理廚房的人，為大眾預備飲食，要運用智慧，要有營養，又合衛生，為大眾服務的功德是無量的。每天要檢查冰箱，容易壞的食物要先吃，不易壞的食物，則妥善保存。不可將食物糟蹋，丟到垃圾桶中，這簡直是造罪業，大家要謹之！慎之！

people rushed back to San Francisco. This is very good.

In the future, whenever there are Dharma assemblies, we should remind people not to talk while they are eating, and not to waste food. We should cherish our food. An ancient verse says,

> As the farmer tills the field
> Under the midday sun,
> His perspiration falls upon the soil;
> Who understands the toil involved
> In producing each grain of rice on the plate?

Most people do not realize how much toil it takes to produce every single grain of rice, so they waste food carelessly. You should understand that people who have nothing to eat now are undergoing the retribution for having wasted food in past lives. I'm telling you this simple principle, so you won't be wasteful.

Those who manage the kitchen should use wisdom in preparing food for the assembly. They should prepare nutritious food in a hygienic manner. By serving the assembly in this way, they can create boundless merit and virtue. The refrigerators need to be checked every day, and perishables should be consumed first. Things that do not spoil easily should be carefully kept. Don't waste food or throw it into the garbage. That is truly creating offenses. Please be careful about this.

管理大眾的飲食，調和恰當，就有功德；若是調和不好，馬馬虎虎，也是有罪過的。立功容易，只看你怎麼去做，合乎法度，就是功；不合乎法度，就是過。總而言之，功過操在做者的手中，愛惜食物，就有功；糟蹋食物，就有過。

一九八三年七月廿四日
開示於萬佛聖城

If the assembly's diet is prepared properly, this will result in merit and virtue. But if it is handled in a sloppy manner, this will result in offenses. If things are done properly and in accord with Dharma, there will be merit; otherwise, there will be offenses. Whether one creates merit or offense depends on oneself. Conserving food creates merit; wasting it creates offenses.

A talk given on July 24, 1983 at
the City of Ten Thousand Buddhas

出版書籍要審查

希望大家盡其所能，
翻譯出無缺點的經，
完全合乎佛意的經。

法界佛教總會、法界佛教大學出版很多佛書，可是還未到盡善盡美的地步。今後無論是誰講的，是誰著的，在未印刷之前，一定要細心審查，經過大家同意，沒有錯誤，再送印刷。

今後，萬佛聖城所有的事情，一律民主作風，大公無私，正直不偏，一切都要求進步，往真善美的方向進行。我們所印行的書籍，不要再有錯誤的地方，如果再有錯誤，對任何人都有影響，還要受人批評，希望大家努力，要做到十全十美的地步。

Carefully Examine Books before Their Publication

Try your best to translate the Sutras flawlessly, in a manner which completely matches the Buddha's intention.

The Dharma Realm Buddhist Association and the Dharma Realm Buddhist University have published many Buddhist books, but these books aren't perfect yet. From now on, no matter who the speaker or author is, all books must be examined carefully and everybody must confirm that there are no errors before the book is printed.

Henceforth, everything at the City of Ten Thousand Buddhas will be done in a democratic manner: by means of selfless, honest and correct procedures. We should try to improve upon and advance towards what is true, good and fair. The books we print should no longer have any errors. If there are errors, this will affect all of us and we'll all be criticized. I hope everyone will try hard to do a perfect job.

37

佛經是釋迦牟尼佛金口所說，一字不能改，一字不能漏，否則不但無功，反而有過。古德說：

依文解義，三世佛冤；
離經一字，即同魔說。

由此可知，翻譯經典不是一件容易的事。希望大家盡其所能，翻譯出無缺點的經，完全合乎佛意的經，流通於世，令讀者受法益。

The Sutras were personally spoken by Shakyamuni Buddha. Not a word can be changed, and not a word can be omitted. Otherwise, there will be no merit but only offenses. The virtuous ones of old said,

> Explaining the meaning too literally
> Grieves the Buddhas of the three times;
> Yet deviating from the Sutra by a single word
> Makes it the same as demonic discourse.

So you know that translating Sutras is not easy. I hope you all will try your best to translate the Sutras flawlessly—in a manner which completely matches the Buddha's intention—and circulate the Sutras throughout the world so that the readers can benefit from the Dharma.

修道要惜福求慧

不可把「福」隨便浪費，
不可把「慧」隨便放棄。

我們佛教徒在沒有成佛之前，應當惜福求慧。惜福
能增長福報，求慧能增長智慧。你們看世上的人，
有種種不同的環境，有的人有很大的福報，不需要
做什麼，便能萬事如意，種種現成，生活富裕，無
憂無慮，快樂無窮，這是因為他在往昔修福修得多
的緣故，所以得到這種大福報。

有的人記憶力特別強，過目不忘，又聰明又健康，
又辯才無礙；說法時，有天花亂墜，地湧金蓮的境
界，為什麼他會這樣子？因為他在往昔修慧修得多
的緣故。怎麼樣修慧？從什麼地方修慧？先從大乘

In Cultivation, Cherish Your Blessings and Seek Wisdom

Don't waste your blessings and neglect wisdom in a careless manner.

Before we Buddhists become Buddhas, we must cherish our blessings and seek wisdom. Fostering blessings increases blessings; seeking wisdom increases wisdom. Look at all the people of the world: they live in different environments. Some, who have great blessings, don't need to work hard to have everything they wish readily available, to have an affluent, carefree life of boundless happiness. That's because in the past they cultivated lots of blessings, so now they have this kind of prosperous reward.

Some people have extraordinarily keen memories. They can retain anything they have glanced at. They are smart, healthy, and eloquent without any impediments in their speech. When they speak Dharma, a golden lotus sprouts from the ground and flowers fall in luxuriant profusion from the sky. Why is this? Because they cultivated lots of

41

經典開始，讀誦大乘經典，把三藏研究得非常透徹，到圓滿的程度，口能背誦，心能思惟，朝於斯，夕於斯，把三藏讀透了，就開大智慧，來生一定又聰明，又有辯才。

我們既然知道惜福求慧的法門，就應該愛物、不糟蹋物質、修橋鋪路、造塔建廟、捨衣施食、救濟貧人，這都是種福田。講經說法、印經流通、翻譯經典、繪畫佛像，這都是修慧的法門。假使你不想有福報，不想有智慧，那就無話可說；若想有福報、有智慧，那麼就趕快修福求慧，不可把福隨便浪費，不可把慧隨便放棄，惜福求慧是佛教徒必行的一件大事。

wisdom in the past. Well, how do we cultivate wisdom? Where do we start? You begin with the Sutras of the Great Vehicle. Recite the Great Vehicle Sutras, learn the Tripitaka until you master it perfectly, so that you can recite it with your mouth and contemplate it with you mind. By being mindful day and night, thoroughly penetrating the Tripitaka, you will develop great wisdom. Then you'll definitely be smart and eloquent in future lives.

Since we know this Dharma-door of fostering blessings and seeking wisdom, we should conserve things and not waste anything. Repairing bridges, paving roads, building stupas and temples, giving clothes and food to the poor—these are all acts of planting fields of blessings. Speaking Dharma, printing and circulating Sutras, translating Sutras, making Buddha images—these are ways of cultivating wisdom. If you don't want blessings or wisdom, there's nothing I can say. But if you do want blessings and wisdom, then quickly cultivate blessings and seek wisdom. Don't waste blessings and neglect wisdom in a careless manner. For Buddhists, fostering blessings and seeking wisdom is a most important task.

脾氣是障道的因緣

不但在外邊沒有脾氣，
就是在內邊也要沒有脾氣。

所謂「煩惱即菩提。」有人問：「不種煩惱，是不是沒有菩提？」不是的，煩惱的本身就是菩提。怎樣是菩提？就是不生煩惱，所以煩惱即菩提。要是只生煩惱，煩惱的本身仍舊是煩惱，菩提仍舊是菩提，大家不要會錯意。

對任何人不可以發脾氣，不但在外邊沒有脾氣，就是在內邊也要沒有脾氣，到了這種境界，才算是真正沒有脾氣的人，敢怒不敢言，那也是發脾氣。偶爾發點小脾氣，無傷大雅，還可以的，但你如果假借名堂，故意發脾氣，那就不對了。

Temper is an Obstacle to the Way

Have no temper not only externally, but also internally.

We say, "Afflictions are Bodhi." Some people ask, "Does this mean that without afflictions there is no Bodhi?" No. Affliction itself is Bodhi. How come? Well, if you don't generate afflictions, then afflictions are Bodhi. If you breed afflictions all the time, then affliction is affliction and Bodhi is Bodhi. Don't get this wrong.

Don't lose your temper at anyone. If you reach the state of having no temper, not only externally but also internally, then you are truly without hostility. If you are angry inside but don't dare to show it, this is also considered losing your temper. If you occasionally lose your temper in some small and harmless way, that's alright. However, if you make excuses about having big fits of temper, that's wrong.

45

如果自己眞正沒有煩惱了，沒有無明了，沒有妄想了，沒有欲念了，到這種境界，雖然有點小脾氣，情有可原，但最好當然是沒有脾氣，與人和睦相處，一團和氣，令人有親切感。

修道人要用德行來感化人，不要用勢力來壓迫人，對任何人要講道理，令人心服口服，眞正佩服你有才幹、有道德、有學問、有慈悲，否則落在名利上，那就離佛道十萬八千里了，這一點要特別謹愼。

出家修道修什麼道？就是修忍辱的道。誰若發脾氣，那就與道相違背，永遠不會與道相感應。發脾氣是一件醜事，是障道的因緣，希望大家謹愼，千萬不要犯這種毛病。

出家修道，沒有把根本的問題抓住，就如同用沙蒸飯，蒸多久的時間，也不會成飯。若是沒有無明火，欲念就會停止，爲什麼？你有欲念，就因爲有火氣，覺得這也不行，那也不行，很多「不行」的問

If you reach a state where you truly have no afflictions, no ignorance, no idle thoughts, and no desires, it would be forgivable to have a little temper. Of course the best thing would be to have no temper at all, and get along harmoniously and amiably with people.

Cultivators should use virtue to teach and transform people, not oppress them with force. Cultivators should be reasonable with everyone. Let people be sincerely convinced, let them respect and admire your ability, virtue, knowledge, and compassion. Otherwise, if you fall for fame and fortune, you'll be a million miles away from Buddhahood. You should be very careful with this.

What is the Way that those who renounce the householder's life cultivate? The Way of patience. Whoever loses his temper is opposing the Way and will never have a response with the Way. Losing your temper is disgraceful. It's an obstacle to the Way. I hope all of you will be cautious and never make this mistake.

Renouncing the householder's life in order to cultivate without understanding the basic questions is like cooking sand in hopes of getting rice. No matter how long you cook it, sand will never become rice. If you didn't have the fire of ignorance, your desires would cease. You have desires because you have this fiery energy. You feel this is wrong and

題跟著來了。所以修道人要把煩惱斷了，才能沒有
一切的麻煩。

一九八三年七月廿五日開示

that isn't right, and as a result there are many more problems. So in order to be free of their troubles, cultivators must cut off afflictions.

A talk given on July 25, 1983 at
the City of Ten Thousand Buddhas

羅漢證道的境界

怎樣能沒有煩惱？方法非常簡單，
就是不爭、不貪、不求、不自私、
不自利、不打妄語。

在《法華經》〈序品第一〉上說：

> 阿羅漢。諸漏已盡。無復煩惱。
> 逮得己利。盡諸有結。心得自在。

這就是羅漢證道的境界。

「諸漏已盡」：諸漏包括多說話、多聽聲、多看色
、多妄想在內。何謂不漏？簡要言之，就是「非禮
勿視，非禮勿聽，非禮勿言，非禮勿動。」這個「
禮」字就是規則，規則也就是戒律。你能非禮勿視

The State of Being Certified to Arhatship

How can one not have any afflictions?
Simply by not fighting, not being greedy,
not seeking, not being selfish,
not pursuing self-benefit, and not lying.

The Introduction to the *Dharma Flower Sutra* says: "[They were] Arhats who had exhausted all outflows and had no further afflictions. Having attained self-benefit, they had exhausted the bonds of all existence and their minds had attained self-mastery." This passage describes the state of Arhats who have certified to the Way. Now I will briefly explain the meaning of the passage:

Exhausted all outflows: Outflows include: talking too much, listening too much, seeing too much, and having too many idle thoughts. What is not having outflows? Simply "not seeing what is improper, not listening to what is improper, not speaking of what is improper, and not acting upon what is improper." Propriety refers to rules, and rules are the same as precepts. Not seeing what is not proper, your eyes

，你的眼根就清淨；你能非禮勿聽，你的耳根就清淨；你能非禮勿言，你的舌根就清淨；你能非禮勿動，你的身根就清淨。六根清淨，就沒有漏。「漏」，好像盛水的器皿，有一個孔，把所盛的水漏掉了，永遠盛不滿水。修道的漏，就是煩惱脾氣，你修點功德，就被無明火燒燬，永遠不能成道業。所以關於這一點，大家要謹慎行事。

在外邊如如不動，在內邊沒有一切欲念，這是沒有漏；在外邊雖然不動，在內邊仍然在動，還是有漏。換句話說，有欲念的思想，有欲念的行為，就是漏；沒有欲念的思想，沒有欲念的行為，就是無漏。修道就是修無漏，修返本還原的功夫，回到童真之體。這些大阿羅漢，諸漏已盡，把渣滓都化盡了，只剩下精華，所以說諸漏已盡。

「無復煩惱」：不會再有煩惱。怎樣能沒有煩惱？方法非常簡單，就是不爭、不貪、不求、不自私、不自利、不打妄語。能這樣子，那就諸漏已盡，煩惱也降伏了。

will be pure; not listening to what is not proper, your ears will be pure; not speaking of what is not proper, your tongue will be pure; not acting upon what is not proper, your body will be pure. Freedom from outflows means the six sense faculties are pure. Having outflows is like having a leak in a container, through which the water leaks out, so that the container never stays full. In cultivation, leaking refers to getting afflicted and losing your temper. You cultivate a little merit and virtue and then turn around and burn it out with the fire of ignorance. You can never succeed in your cultivation like this. You should all be very careful in this matter.

To be "thus, thus, unmoving" externally and free of all desires internally, is to have no outflows. If you are externally composed yet moved internally, you still have outflows. In other words, having acts or thoughts of desire is the same as having outflows; not having them is not having outflows. Cultivating the Way means becoming free from outflows and developing the skills of returning to the source and regaining one's purity. These great Arhats have burned off the extraneous matter and kept only the essence, so they are said to have exhausted all outflows.

Had no further afflictions: How can one not have any afflictions? Simply by not fighting, not being greedy, not seeking, not being selfish, not pursuing self-benefit, and not lying. Since the Arhats are like this, they have exhausted all outflows and subdued all afflictions.

「逮得己利」：他們得到禪悅爲食，法喜充滿的利益，得到無諍三昧，把勝負心停止了。

所謂：

> 諍是勝負心，與道相違背；
> 便生四相心，由何得三昧？

「盡諸有結」：「有」，是三界二十五有；「結」，是爲煩惱而結集生死。有見惑、思惑、塵沙惑、無明惑，就障礙我們出離三界。如果把習氣毛病剷除，把結集在一起的煩惱沒有了，把三有種種的問題也沒有了，這就盡諸有結，了了分段生死。

「心得自在」：爲什麼能這樣？因爲心中得到快樂自在的緣故。爲什麼心得自在？因爲諸漏已盡，無復煩惱，逮得己利，盡諸有結的關係，諸大羅漢已到諸漏已盡，梵行已立，所作已辦，不受後有的境界。

Having attained self-benefit: They have attained the benefit of "taking the bliss of Dhyana for food and being filled with the joy of the Dharma." They have all attained the samadhi of non-contention; they have extinguished thoughts of winning and losing. It is said, "Contention involves notions of winning and losing. This goes against the Way and gives rise to the mind of the four characteristics. How can one attain samadhi this way?"

Had exhausted the bonds of all existence: Existence refers to the twenty-five kinds of existence in the Three Realms. Bonds refer to being bound by birth and death due to afflictions. View-delusions, thought-delusions, delusions like dust and sand, and the delusion of ignorance prevent living beings from leaving the Three Realms. If we can eradicate all our bad habits and faults, break all the bonds of affliction, and dissolve all the problems of the Three Realms, we have exhausted the bonds of all existence and ended share-section birth and death.

Their minds had attained self-mastery: How could they do this? Because their minds have attained happiness and freedom. How have their minds attained self-mastery? Because they have exhausted all outflows, have no further afflictions, have attained self-benefit, and have exhausted the bonds of all existence. These great Arhats have exhausted all outflows, have established pure conduct, and have done what they had to do, and so they will undergo no further becoming.

我們的心，都是「他在」而不是「自在」。「他在」就是人雖在，可是心不在，不是想南朝，就是想北國，不是念東西，就是念南北，始終沒有停止的時候。我們妄想紛飛把主人翁攆跑了，外邊的客塵來當家，所以心不自在。「自在」就是心無雜念，自性放大光明，照天照地，身心清淨，逍遙自在。

這幾句經文非常要緊，我們要記住，不可忘失，把它研究明白了，保證能了生脫死，同羅漢的境界一樣。不證羅漢果，心不會自在；證了羅漢果，把客塵趕走，把煩惱降伏了，這時心才得到自在。

Our mind has no self-mastery because it is controlled by "otherness." When our body is here but our mind isn't, it's a case of being controlled by something else. If the mind isn't thinking of the south, it's thinking of the north; if it's not thinking of east and west, then it's thinking of south and north. It never stops. The random thoughts swirl around. They kick out the host and let the external guest-dust rule. Thus the mind has no self-mastery. To attain self-mastery means having no random thoughts. Then the self-nature emits a bright light which illumines heaven and earth. Both body and mind are pure, free, and at ease.

This is a very important passage—please remember it. Study it until you understand, and then I can assure you that you will end birth and death, just like the Arhats. Before we have proven the results of Arhatship, our minds are not free. Only after we have certified to Arhatship, expelled the guest-dust, and subdued afflictions can we attain self-mastery.

為什麼要念佛？

平時念佛，
就是為臨終時作一個準備。

為什麼我們平時要念佛呢？平時念佛，就是為臨終時作一個準備。為什麼不等到臨終時才念呢？因為習慣是日積月累而成的。你平時沒有念佛的習慣，等到臨命終時，就想不起來要念佛，或根本不知道要念佛。所以平時要學著念佛，修淨土法門，等到臨命終時才不會驚慌失措，而得以平安往生極樂世界。

為什麼要往生西方極樂世界？因為阿彌陀佛在因地，為法藏比丘時，曾發四十八大願，其中說，我成

Why Recite the Buddha's Name?

Reciting the Buddha's name in ordinary times prepares us for our final hour.

Why do we recite the Buddha's name in ordinary times? Reciting in ordinary times prepares us for our final hour. Why don't we wait until the last hour to recite? Because habits are formed by gradually through the days and months. If you're not in the habit of reciting at ordinary times, at your last moment you won't remember to recite, or won't even know what to recite. So it's important to practice reciting the Buddha's name and cultivate the Pure Land Dharma-door on a regular basis. Then you won't panic at the time of death, and you'll be able to attain peaceful rebirth in the Land of Ultimate Bliss.

Why do we want to get reborn in the Land of Ultimate Bliss? Because when Amitabha Buddha was the Bhikshu Fazang (Dharma Treasury) in a past life, he made forty-

佛之後，十方所有的眾生，若有稱念我名號者，我一定接引他到我的世界來，將來成佛。在我的世界裏，眾生都是由蓮華化生，故身體清淨無染。因爲阿彌陀佛發這種大願，所以一切眾生都應該修念佛法門，這是很對機，很容易修的一個法門。

在經上又說：

> 末法人修行，一億人修行，
> 罕一得道，唯以念佛得度。

這就是說一億人修行，一個得道的都沒有，只有念佛才能往生極樂世界而得度。尤其現在末法時代，念佛正與一般人的根機相應。

但在西方，現在不是末法時代，可以說是正法時代。爲什麼說是正法時代？因爲佛法剛剛傳到西方國家來，正當興旺。所以現在美國有很多人歡喜參禪打坐，這也是正法的表現。在正法時期也可修念佛法門，末法時期也可以修念佛法門，什麼時代都可

eight great vows. In one of these vows he said, "After I have become a Buddha, if there are living beings in the ten directions who recite my name, I will receive them and bring them to my land, and they will become Buddhas in the future. In my land, all living beings are born transformationally from lotus flowers, so their bodies will be pure and have no defilement." Because of these great vows made by Amitabha Buddha, all living beings should cultivate the Dharma-door of reciting the Buddha's name. This is a very appropriate and easy Dharma-door to cultivate. The Sutras also say,

"In the Dharma-ending Age, it will be rare even for one out of a hundred million cultivators to attain the Way. Only by reciting the Buddha's name can living beings be saved."

Only those who recite the Buddha's name can be reborn in the Land of Ultimate Bliss. Reciting the Buddha's name is especially appropriate for people in the present Dharma-ending Age.

However, in the West, it's not the Dharma-ending Age right now. It's the Proper Dharma Age, because the Buddhadharma has just been transmitted to the West, and it has just started to flourish. Therefore, many Americans like to sit in meditation and investigate Chan. This is an indication of the Proper Dharma Age. During the Proper Dharma Age, people can also cultivate the Dharma-door of reciting the Buddha's name, as

以修行，如果有人對其他法門，功夫用不上，可以
修念佛法門。

永明壽大師說：「有禪有淨土，猶如帶角虎；現世
爲人師，將來作佛祖。」又參禪又念佛，好像老虎
有犄角似的；現世可以爲人的師表，將來可以成佛
作祖。

所以眞正參禪的人，就是眞正念佛；眞正念佛的人
，也就是眞正參禪。再深一層地說，眞正持戒的人
，也就是眞正參禪；眞正參禪的人，也就是眞正持
戒。那麼眞正講經說法的人，他是爲講經而講經，
也就是眞正參禪。

《永嘉大師證道歌》上說：

> 宗亦通，說亦通，
> 定慧圓明不滯空。

又會參禪，又會講經，這是宗說兼通。再進一層說
，眞正持咒的人，眞正修密宗的人，也就是眞正參
禪。

can people in the Dharma-ending Age. In fact, people of all ages can cultivate this Dharma-door. If people have difficulty developing their skills in other Dharma-doors, they can cultivate the Dharma-door of reciting the Buddha's name.

Great Master Yongming Shou said, "With Chan and with Pure Land, one is like a tiger wearing horns—in this life a teacher of people, in the future a patriarch and a Buddha."

One who truly investigates Chan is really reciting the Buddha's name, and one who really recites is truly investigating Chan. Let me explain further: one who truly upholds the precepts is really investigating Chan, and one who really investigates Chan is truly upholding the precepts. A true Sutra lecturer who speaks Sutras for the sake of speaking Sutras is also truly investigating Chan. The "Song of Enlightenment" by Great Master Yongjia says:

> The (Chan) school and the doctrines
>   are both mastered;
> Samadhi and wisdom are completely clear;
> I do not stagnate in emptiness.

One who is capable of investigating Chan and explaining Sutras has mastered both the practice of Chan and the doctrines. Further, one who truly recites mantras, a true cultivator of the esoteric school, is also truly investigating Chan.

禪、教、淨、律、密，雖說五種，歸根究底說的都是一個，沒有兩個。其實再深一層說，連一個也沒有，怎麼會有五個呢？真正學佛法的人，在這一點上應該明白。所以有的人有門户之見，認為念佛法門最高，參禪不對；或者有人說參禪最高，念佛錯誤，這都是沒有明白佛法的人。應知一切皆是佛法，皆不可得，既無法可得，何必又在頭上安頭呢？何必無事找事做呢？你若真明白法了，無法可得。可是對一些不明白法的人，你對他說「根本什麼也沒有。」他就會失望。所以佛說「權法」，就是為了說「實法」；說「權智」，為的是「實智」。實智是什麼呢？實智是一個「歸無所得」。實相無相，無所不相，這才是真實的智慧。

Although there are the five schools (Chan, Doctrines, Vinaya [Ethics], Esoteric, and Pure Land), fundamentally there is only one. Actually, if we take it one step further, there isn't even one, so how could there be five? A person who is truly studying Buddhism should be very clear about this. People with sectarian prejudices may think that the Dharma-door of reciting the Buddha's name is the best and investigating Chan isn't right, or others may say investigating Chan is the best and reciting the Buddha's name is a mistake. These people haven't understood the Buddhadharma yet. We should be aware that it's all Buddhadharma, all equally unattainable. Since there is no dharma to be attained, why add a head on top of a head? Why look for something to do when there's nothing to be done? If you truly understand the Dharma, there isn't a dharma to be attained. However, if you tell people who don't understand the Dharma that there is nothing, they will be very disappointed. So the Buddha used provisional Dharma in order to speak the actual Dharma; he spoke expedient wisdom for the sake of real wisdom. What is real wisdom? Real wisdom is "returning to attaining nothing." Absolute reality has no characteristics, and yet it characterizes everything. This is true and real wisdom.

人應該盡孝道嗎？

修行人，能把父母放下，
專心一致修行，這是對的。
既然不修行，也不盡孝道，這是不對的。

今天我們大家來研究這個問題：「就是人為什麼要孝順父母？應該孝順父母，還是不應該孝順父母？」這個問題，有兩種解釋。

站在「出世間法」的立場來講，不應該孝順父母。我相信任何人聽過這句話，一定大吃一驚，因為從來沒有聽過這種話。你所知道的是人人應該孝順父母，沒有聽過人說不應該盡孝道這句話，所以你覺得驚奇。若按照真理來講，是這樣的說法。若是站在「世間法」的立場來講，當然應該孝順父母。世

Should One Practice Filiality?

If cultivators can let go of their parents and immerse themselves in cultivation, they are on the right track. But if one neither cultivates nor is filial to one's parents, one is on the wrong path.

Today, let's investigate the question: should one be filial to one's parents, and why? There are two sides to this question.

From the viewpoint of world-transcending Dharma, we shouldn't be filial to our parents. I believe that anyone listening to this is shocked, because this idea is unheard of. You know that one should be filial to one's parents; you have never heard of a view stating that one shouldn't practice filiality. That's why you are surprised. Yet, if we speak according to true principle, this view is correct. But from the worldly point of view, of course we should be filial to our parents. The worldly point of view says that just as a tree has its roots and a stream has its source, we also have our roots and we should pay attention to them. We should

間法是木本水源，應該慎終追遠、孝順父母、恭敬師長，這是天經地義之事。

若按出世法來講，我們努力修行，用功學習，發大菩提心，就是盡大孝，而不是小孝。此話怎麼解釋？因爲修行有所成就，可以超度七世父母升天，所謂：「一子成道，九祖升天。」這就是大孝。

孝有四種：一爲大孝，二爲小孝，三爲遠孝，四爲近孝。什麼是大孝？就是報生生世世的父母恩、師長恩。什麼是小孝？就是孝順現世的父母，膝下承歡，令父母高興。養父母的身、慰父母的心，也就是要恭敬父母、供養父母。什麼是遠孝？就是孝敬古聖先賢，效法他們的一言一行，作爲借鏡；一舉一動，作爲圭臬。什麼是近孝？就是除了孝順自己父母之外，還要孝順他人的父母，所謂「老吾老，以及人之老」，要有這種的思想和行爲。

真正出世法，超過孝道，所以我方才說：「不應該執著孝。」若是執著孝順父母，那就沾上情情愛愛

always carefully attend to the funeral rites of our parents and to the worship of our ancestors. We should be filial towards our parents, and respectful towards our teachers and elders. All this is a matter of course.

However, according to world-transcending Dharma, if we cultivate diligently, work hard at learning, and bring forth a great Bodhi mind, this is great filiality, not small filiality. How is that? When you have accomplishment in cultivation, you can rescue your parents from your past seven lives and help them to be reborn in the heavens. It is said, "When one child becomes a Buddha, Ancestors of the past nine lives Ascend to the heavens." This is great filiality.

There are four types of filiality: great, small, distant, and close. *Great filiality* means repaying the kindness of one's parents, teachers, and elders from all lives. *Small filiality* is filiality towards one's parents of this present life, making them happy, providing food and shelter for them, and giving them peace of mind. It means respecting one's parents and providing for them. *Distant filiality* refers to respecting and being filial to the ancient sages and worthy ones, taking them as models and emulating their words and conduct . *Close filiality* is, in addition to being filial to one's own parents, also being filial to other people's parents. It is to "take care of your own elders and extend the same care to others." This is how we should think and behave.

True world-transcending Dharma surpasses filiality. That's

的思想，就有妄念，終日念父思母，焉能修道？所以按真理來講，不應該盡孝道。

我講這個道理，有人會懂，有人會不懂，所以大家要深一層研究這個問題。

現在的人心，一天比一天壞，品行一天比一天惡劣，所謂「人心不古」。為什麼？因為世間人，本應該孝順父母，可是他不孝順父母。認為孝順父母是落伍的思想，又認為父母養育兒女，是他應盡的責任而已。那麼，他不盡孝道，是不是修行呢？也不是的。他真能修行，不需要養父母，也算是孝順父母，這是盡大孝，將來超度父母生天。他既不孝順父母，也不修行，專造種種的惡業，將來一定墮落三惡道，毫無疑問。

你們看！現在的青年男女，學下流的行為，不是殺人放火，就是姦婬劫盜，無惡不為。覺得應該這樣放蕩不羈，以為自由。他認為人不應該孝順父母，就應該學壞，這種思想，大錯特錯。雖然不能一概

why I say, "Don't get attached to filiality." If you're attached to filiality, you are still caught up in love and emo-
tion. You're always thinking of your parents. How can you
cultivate this way? Therefore, according to true principle
one should not be filial to one's parents. Some of you may
understand the principle I'm talking about, and others may
not. So we need to investigate further.

At present, people's minds are getting worse day by day,
and their behavior is getting daily more wicked. It is said,
"People's minds are no longer like the the minds of the
ancients." People ought to be filial to their parents but they
aren't. They think filiality is an outdated idea, and they
think raising children is the parents' obligation. So then, if a
person doesn't practice filiality, does that mean they are
cultivating? Of course not. If a person could truly cultivate,
even if he didn't provide for his parents, he would still be
considered filial. This is great filial piety, helping one's
parents be reborn in the heavens. If a person neither practices filiality nor cultivates, but only creates all kinds of evil
karma, then he will definitely fall into the three evil paths.
There is no question about it.

You can see present-day young men and women learning
despicable behavior. If it's not killing and arson, then it's
robbery and promiscuity. They do every evil thing there is
to do, and they call their lack of restraint, "freedom." They
think that not being filial to one's parents means one should
learn to be bad. This kind of thinking is absolutely wrong.

而論，但是大致差不多是犯了這種通病。

修行人，雖然不孝順父母，可是能拯救父母離苦海，生於天界。但有些人，既不孝順父母，又不修行，終日做些不道德的事，有害於家庭，擾亂社會、國家，不得安寧。這是賠本的生意，越賠越沒有底，前途不堪設想。這樣胡作非為，乃是不可寬恕的罪人。

在前邊所說的修行人，能把父母放下，專心一致修行，這是對的。既然不修行，也不盡孝道，這是不對的。這一點要弄清楚，所謂：

　　萬惡婬為首，百善孝為先。

　　　　　　　　一九八三年七月二十九日
　　　　　　　　觀音七開示於萬佛聖城

Even though we cannot generalize, many people have this fault.

A cultivator, although he can't be filial to his parents, can save his parents from the sea of suffering and help them to ascend to the heavens. However, some people neither practice filiality nor do they cultivate. They only commit immoral acts, which ruin families and disrupt society, causing there to be no peace in the nation. Such behavior is a losing business: the more you lose, the less capital you have left, and your future is doomed. People who act this stupidly are inexcusable offenders.

On the other hand, if one is like the cultivator mentioned above and can let go of one's parents and immerse oneself in cultivation, then one is on the right track. But if one neither cultivates nor is filial to one's parents, one is on the wrong path. You should be clear about this. It is said,

> Lust is the worst of all evils.
> Filiality is the foremost of all virtues.

A talk given on July 29, 1983,
at the City of Ten Thousand Buddhas

何謂善知識

善知識依照佛法修行，
惡知識依照魔法修行。

淺言之，善知識就是有智慧的人，惡知識就是愚癡
的人。善知識有正知正見，惡知識有邪知邪見。合
乎佛法就是正知正見，不合乎佛法就是邪知邪見。
善知識依照佛法修行，惡知識依照魔法修行，善惡
的關鍵在這個地方來分別。

善知識用「四攝法」來教化人。何謂四攝法？就是
布施、愛語、利行、同事。這四種法容易和眾生打
成一片，令眾生對於佛法發生興趣，深信佛法。

What Is a Good Advisor?

A good advisor cultivates in accord with the Buddhadharma; an evil advisor cultivates in accord with demonic dharma.

A good advisor is someone with wisdom; an evil advisor is an ignorant person. A good advisor has proper knowledge and views; an evil advisor has deviant knowledge and views. Proper knowledge and views accord with the Buddhadharma; deviant knowledge and views do not. A good advisor cultivates in accord with the Buddhadharma, an evil advisor cultivates in accord with demonic dharma. These are the criteria that differentiate good and evil.

A good advisor teaches and transforms people with the Four Methods of Conversion: giving, kind words, beneficial conduct, and cooperation. With these four methods, you can get along easily with living beings, inspiring their interest and eventually their deep faith in the Buddhadharma.

1. Giving: For people to have a good impression of us and

（一）布施：要想令人相信佛法，必須布施財和法給他，令他對你發生好感。

（二）愛語：就是不違背人情，不違背佛法，說些慈愛的話。

（三）利行：隨起身口意行，令眾生各霑法益。

（四）同事：對於應度的眾生與他做同樣的工作。

這四種法，是聯絡感情的方法。你能言行一致，大公無私，以身作則，見義勇為。眾生自然相信你所說的話，也就相信佛法是度生死海的寶筏。

你們來到這裏聽經研究佛法，都是有大知識的人。要知道菩提自性本是清淨的。本來清淨，就是一法不立，一塵不染，不假造作，本來現前，本來具足。這個菩提自性，也就是佛性。這一點，各位要特別注意！

to enable them to believe in the Buddhadharma, we give them both wealth and Dharma.

2. Kind words: We speak kindly, following the principle of not going against human feelings or against the Buddhadharma.

3. Beneficial conduct: With our body, mouth and mind, we bring the benefits of Dharma to living beings.

4. Cooperation: We work alongside the same living beings we want to liberate.

These four methods are means to get in touch with and develop rapport with living beings. If you always do what you say, are selfless, set an example with your own conduct, and bravely do what's right, then living beings will naturally believe what you say and will also believe that the Buddhadharma is a precious vessel for crossing the ocean of birth and death.

You people who come here to listen to Sutra lectures and investigate the Buddhadharma are all great learned ones. You should know that the inherent, enlightened nature is fundamentally clear and pure. Within the inherent nature not a single dharma is established, nor is it defiled by any dust. This nature is not produced; it is fundamentally apparent and fundamentally complete. This enlightened nature is the Buddha-nature. Everyone pay close attention to this!

每個人的佛性和諸佛是一樣，沒有什麼分別。不過，我們太愚癡，被無明妄想所覆蓋，所以佛性不現前。若能用智慧來處理一切事情，佛性現前，那就是善知識。

Everyone's Buddha-nature is the same as that of all Buddhas. There is no difference. But because we are too deluded, shrouded by ignorance and idle thoughts, the Buddha-nature fails to manifest. If we could use wisdom to handle all of our affairs, our Buddha-nature would manifest, and we would be good advisors.

如人飲水，冷暖自知

打七不是隨梆唱影，
敷衍了事，來湊熱鬧。

這次觀音七已經圓滿了。每個人要把自己感應的境界向大眾報告，給大眾作爲借鏡。念觀世音菩薩聖號，有什麼感應？有什麼境界？或者開了智慧？或者斷了煩惱？或者破了執著？所謂「如人飲水，冷暖自知」。每個人自己知道，外人不曉得。

各位要曉得打七不是隨梆唱影，敷衍了事，來湊熱鬧。而是剋期取證，分秒必爭的用功，一點也不能馬虎。在這七天之中，或者見到菩薩現光，或者見到現華，或者感覺身心輕安愉快等等，這些都是境界。

Only the Drinker of the Water Knows its Temperature

You should be aware that attending a session is not something you can be perfunctory about, or just join in for fun.

This Guanyin session has been completed. Each of you should relate to the assembly any states or responses you've had, so the assembly can learn from your experiences. What kinds of responses did you have from reciting Guanyin Bodhisattva's holy name? What states did you have? Have you developed wisdom? Have you severed all afflictions? Have you broken through attachments? It's said, "In drinking water, only the drinker knows its temperature." People know for themselves what others do not. Attending a session is not something you can be perfunctory about, or just join in for fun. To achieve something in the limited time available, you have to work hard, strive every second, not be casual. During these seven days, people may have seen Bodhisattvas emitting light, or flowers appearing, or felt a happiness and a light ease in their bodies and minds. These are all states.

多用功少説話

大家在這裏埋頭苦幹，
認真修行。

凡是參加佛七也好，禪七也好，觀音七也好，地藏七也好，不可向外宣傳萬佛聖城如何好。萬佛聖城的好處不希望外人知道。萬佛聖城是默默經營，大家在這裏埋頭苦幹，認真修行，所以不注重對外宣傳。你們在這裏覺得好，可以繼續來；覺得不好，這條路就不要再走——這是萬佛聖城一貫的宗旨。

萬佛聖城立六大宗旨，作爲修行的目標；就是「不爭、不貪、不求、不自私、不自利、不妄語。」你們能明白六大宗旨的眞實義，那就沒有白到萬佛聖城一趟。

Work Harder, Talk Less

People here immerse themselves in their own work and cultivate earnestly.

Whether you have come here to attend a recitation session, a Chan session, a Guanyin session, or an Earth Store Bodhisattva session, you should not advertise how nice the City of Ten Thousand Buddhas is. We don't want people outside to know the nice things about the City. Here at the City, we work quietly. People here immerse themselves in their own work and cultivate earnestly. We don't care about advertising ourselves to the outside world. If you feel this is a good place, you can come again; if you feel this place is not so good, then you can stop coming. This is the City's principle.

As guidelines for cultivation, the City has established Six Guidelines. They are: no fighting, no greed, no seeking, no selfishness, no pursuit of self-benefit, and no lying. If you can understand the true meaning of these guidelines, you have not come here in vain.

一般人歡喜好名，但萬佛聖城不需要。為什麼？因萬佛聖城的宗旨是將財色名食睡這五欲斷絕。這五欲乃是地獄五條根，一般人歡喜它，可是萬佛聖城要和它脫離關係，所以萬佛聖城不需要什麼好名，不企求什麼利益，就本著真實的功夫來弘揚佛法，續佛慧命，這是萬佛聖城大概的情況。

Ordinary people like fame, but the City doesn't need it. At the City the ideal is to cut off the five desires, that is, the desires for wealth, sex, fame, food and sleep. These five desires are the five roots of hell. Ordinary people take pleasure in them, but we at the City want to sever our relationship with them. The City doesn't crave a famous reputation or seek any benefits. We only use our real skills to propagate the Buddhadharma and continue the Buddha's wisdom life. That is how things are at the City.

參禪要念茲在茲

「不到開悟不罷休」，
要有這種金剛的願力。

這次禪七剛開始，希望大家聚精會神來參禪，拿出勇氣來參禪，念茲在茲來參禪。總之，要拿出「了生脫死，發憤忘食」的精神；「不到開悟不罷休」，要有這種金剛的願力。

若能有人罵你，你沒聽見；有人打你，你也無感覺；有沒有吃飯都不知道；有沒有睡覺都不知道。如果到了這種境界，轉過身來，就知道以前都是在皮毛上用功夫，到今天才真正知道應該做些什麼。

禪七開始，我對大家說幾句粗淺的話，要是能明白

Investigating Chan, One Must Be Mindful

Don't give up until you have reached enlightenment. You must have adamantine will power.

This Chan session has just begun. I hope you will concentrate your attention and energy to investigate Chan, to be mindful in your investigation. You should be so determined to end birth and death that you even forget about eating. Don't give up until you have reached enlightenment. You must have adamantine will power.

When you reach the state where you don't hear it when people scold you, don't feel it when people beat you, and don't even know if you have eaten or slept, then you can look back and know that everything you did in the past was inconsequential and that only today do you really know what you need to do.

At the beginning of this Chan session, I will say a few introductory words to you. If you understand, they will be

，就有很大的幫助；若是不明白，也有很大的幫助。有人問：「怎麼樣幫助呢？」我現在不能告訴你。如果告訴你，你明白之後，就在那裏障住了，不能進步。現在把這幾句說出來，希望你們注意聽：

> 梵語禪那波羅蜜，此云靜慮細進參；
> 山高水深無所畏，始知天外別有天。

「禪定」在印度話叫作「禪那波羅蜜」。這個法門修行到圓滿時，便可到彼岸。在中國譯爲「靜慮」，又叫「思惟修」。可是靜慮和思惟修，要仔細地追究，要詳細地鑽參。參什麼？參「念佛是誰？」的話頭。就是上高山、入深海也不怕，這時候，才知天外還有重重無盡的天。所以要綿綿細細地參，念茲在茲地參，參來參去，參到「山窮水盡疑無路」時，一轉身就是「柳岸花明又一村」的境界。

一九八三年七月三十一日
禪七開示於萬佛聖城

88

a great help. If you don't understand, they will also be a great help. Someone may ask, "How can this be?" Well, I cannot tell you now. If I told you, then after you understood it, you would get stuck there and wouldn't advance. Now let me read you a verse. I hope you'll listen carefully:

> The Sanskrit words *dhyana paramita*
> Mean to contemplate in stillness and subtly advance
>   your investigation.
> Have no fear of high mountains or deep waters;
> Then you will discover the sky beyond the sky.

In Sanskrit, Chan samadhi is called *dhyana paramita*. When you cultivate this Dharma-door to perfection, you can reach the other shore. In Chinese it is translated as "still contemplation," or "mental cultivation." In still contemplation and mental cultivation, you need to investigate carefully and in detail. Investigate what? Investigate the topic of "Who is reciting the Buddha's name?" Don't be afraid of ascending the high mountains or descending into the depths of the sea; at this time you will find there are myriad layers of heavens beyond heavens. Therefore, investigate continuously, extensively, and mindfully; investigate back and forth until "the mountains disappear and waters vanish, and there is no road ahead." At that time, you turn around and enter the state where "in the shade of the willows, bright flowers bloom and there is yet another village."

A talk given on July 31, 1983,
at the City of Ten Thousand Buddhas

為何與道不相應

就是因為我們有個虛妄不實的「妄心」。

太上老君《清靜經》上說：

「眾生所以不得真道者，為有妄心。

　　既有妄心，即驚其神。

　　既驚其神，即著萬物。

　　既著萬物，即生貪求。

　　既生貪求，即是煩惱。

　　煩惱妄想，憂苦身心。

　　便遭濁辱，流浪生死，

　　常沉苦海，永失真道。

Why Do We Lose the True Way?

Because we are using the false mind.

The *Classic of Eternal Purity and Stillness*, by the High Master Lao Zi, says:

> Why do living beings fail to obtain the True Way?
> Because they have false thoughts.
> With false thoughts, the spirit is disturbed.
> Once the spirit is disturbed,
> It attaches to external things.
> Attaching to external things produces greed.
> Greed leads to affliction.
> Afflictions and false thinking in turn
> Trouble and vex both body and mind.
> Thus they meet with foul disgrace and
> Wander in birth and death,
> Constantly immersed in the sea of suffering and
> Forever losing the True Way.

　　真常之道，悟者自得。

　　得悟道者，常清靜矣。」

我們無論用什麼功，也不能與道相應，總是不上路，這是什麼原因？就是因為我們有個虛妄不實的「妄心」。好高騖遠，求名求利，這都是妄心。有了妄心，對於自性就有動搖，好像一桶水，不動時，沙泥沉底，則水清淨；若是用棒子（妄心）把水攪拌成濁水，那麼就不辨真假、不分善惡，這時，擇法眼也不具足，智慧也不現前。

「水濁不清」，就著住在萬物，亂七八糟，找不出頭緒，為什麼？因為著住在萬物上，便生貪求心，認為萬物是真實的。貪求心生出來，就有煩惱。貪求到也煩惱，貪求不到也煩惱，因為煩惱和妄想交織在一起，就被五濁惡世的濁埋沒了，那就不能恢復清淨，因為這樣，所以生了又死，死了又生，生生不息，永無了期。生的時候，不知道是怎樣生的，所以糊塗；死的時候，不知道怎樣死的，還是糊塗。不但生時糊塗，死時糊塗，就是活著，也是糊

The true and everlasting Way is attained
By those who are awakened.
Those who awaken to the Way
Are eternally pure and calm.

When people work hard in their cultivation yet don't have a response, it is because they are using the false mind to seek what is lofty and distant. For example, when people seek fame and profit, the false mind is at work. The false mind disturbs the intrinsic nature. It is like a pail of water gradually becoming clear as the silt and sand sink to the bottom. But when the water is stirred up, it becomes turbid again. When we use our false mind, we muddy the water of our intrinsic nature, and we are unable to distinguish between true and false. We lack Dharma-selecting vision and our wisdom doesn't come forth. We become unclear just like that muddy water.

When we become attached to external things, everything gets all muddled and confused and we can't find our way out. Our minds turn to greed (because we think everything external is real), and this greedy mind is the source of our afflictions. If we get what we seek, we are afflicted; and if we don't get what we seek, we are still afflicted. When the mind gets tangled up in afflictions and false thoughts, it drowns in the muddy river of the evil world of five turbidities, and cannot return to purity. For that very reason we are born and we die; we die and are then reborn. At birth we are unaware of how we got here; when we die, we don't know the reason for our death. Not only are we muddled at the time of birth

塗。糊塗一輩子，也沒有弄清楚，所以流浪生死，就把眞心丟了。眞心遺失，就掉到苦海中，爬不出來。若能明白這種道理，就是開悟。不會被虛妄不實的境界所轉，而智慧即時現前。有了智慧，就不顛倒。

在《楞嚴經》上說：「狂心頓歇，歇即菩提。」我們爲什麼和道不相應呢？就因爲「狂心」沒有休息。這個狂心，就是不滿現實的心，也就是貪而無厭的心，也就是有憎有愛的心。若把這種心停止，就是智慧，就是覺道，就是佛性的本體。可是我們把這個眞理忽略了。所以在糊塗境界上，處之泰然，悠哉游哉，不想辦法出離三界的生死苦海。

and death, we are muddled all during our lives, and we never become clear. We have been wandering in birth and death and have lost our true mind. Since the true mind is lost, we fall into the sea of suffering and are unable to get out. If we can understand this principle, we can get enlightened. Then we won't be turned by false states. Our wisdom will come forth, and we won't be confused anymore.

The *Shurangama Sutra* says, "When the mad mind stops, that very stopping is Bodhi." Why don't we have any response in the Way? Because the mad mind has not stopped. This mad mind is dissatisfied with the way things are; it is insatiable-it is the mind of love and hate. If we can put this mind to rest, then we have wisdom; we have the enlightened Way, the substance of the Buddha-nature. But in fact we have ignored this principle. We wallow in our muddled state, feeling perfectly at ease, and make no attempt to escape from the bitter ocean of birth and death.

講經說法要謹慎

學佛法的人，不要圖快，
要細嚼慢嚥，品其滋味。

無論是出家人，或是在家人，在講經說法的時候，
一定要十分小心。事前要靜坐五分鐘，將心安定之
後，再翻開經本，合掌恭恭敬敬地讀誦經文，然後
詳細地解釋。如果對理論不相應，勉強解說，就不
合乎邏輯學。

所以講經或說法，先要把「名相」弄清楚，先要把
「經文的義理」搞明白，否則就很容易講錯，所謂
「差之絲毫，謬之千里。」令聽經的人，得不到要
領，有莫名其妙之感。

96

Be Prudent When Speaking the Dharma and Lecturing on the Sutras

Students of Buddhism should not try to hurry. We should take our time in savoring the flavor of the food we eat.

Whether you are a monk or nun or a lay person, you must be very careful when you speak the Dharma or lecture on the Sutras. Before you start your talk, sit quietly for five minutes. After your mind is calmed down, open the Sutra, put your palms together and reverently read the Sutra text, and then explain it in detail. If you don't quite understand the principles of the Sutra, you won't be able to give a coherent explanation.

Therefore before speaking Dharma or giving Sutra lectures, you must be clear about all the terms, and understand the principles and meanings of the Sutra text. Otherwise it's very easy to make mistakes. It is said, "If you are off by a hair in the beginning, you'll miss it by a thousand miles in the end." You'll end up confusing your listeners.

學佛法的人，不要圖快，所謂「囫圇吞棗，食而不知其味。」要細嚼慢嚥，品其滋味。貪多嚼不爛，反而受其害。講經要注意經的義理，稍有講錯，便與整個經義不相吻合，不但沒有功德，反而有罪過，所謂：

依文解義，三世佛怨；
離經一字，即同魔說。

後果多麼嚴重，謹之！慎之！

至於聽經的人，更要聚精會神地聽，不管講經的法師或居士所講的經或所說的法，講得好，也應該注意聽；講得不好，更要注意聽。要研究，講得好，好在什麼地方？講得不好，不好在什麼地方？好的，就學習；不好的，要改正過來，作為自己的借鏡，這樣才能鍛鍊自己的擇法眼。

擇法眼是從修戒、修定、修慧三方面而來。戒定慧圓融無礙，則對於一切經藏，迎刃而解，沒有絲毫

Students of Buddhism should not try to hurry. That would be like "swallowing a date without chewing, eating it without knowing its taste." We should take our time in savoring the flavor of the food we eat. If we are greedy and bite off more than we can chew, it will be harmful to us. When you are lecturing, pay attention to the meaning and principle of the Sutra. If you make a small mistake, your lecture will not match the meaning of the entire Sutra. In that case, you'll create offenses instead of acquiring any merit. It is said,

> Explaining the meaning too literally
> Grieves the Buddhas of the three periods of time;
> Yet deviating from the Sutra by a single word
> Makes it the same as demonic discourse.

What a serious consequence! One must be very cautious!

As for people who listen to the Sutra lectures, you should concentrate your attention and energy and listen, regardless of whether the Dharma Master or layperson speaks well or not. You should look into why they speak well or poorly. Then you can learn from their good points and use their weak points as examples to correct your own shortcomings. This way you'll be able to develop your Dharma-selecting vision.

Dharma-selecting vision comes from cultivating precepts, samadhi, and wisdom. When precepts, samadhi and wisdom are perfectly fused with no obstruction, then you'll be able to understand all the Sutras and Shastras effortlessly,

的障礙。這時候，講經說法，口若懸河，滔滔不絕，沒有窮盡。古人講經，有天花亂墜，地湧金蓮的境界，你們雖然沒有這種境界，可是也要有樂說無礙之辯才。

一九八三年八月十一日
開示於萬佛聖城

without the slightest hindrance. At that point, you will be eloquent in speaking Dharma and lecturing on the Sutras. When the ancients lectured on the Sutras, flowers would rain from the sky and golden lotuses would come forth from the earth. Even if you don't quite reach this state, with Dharma-selecting vision you will have unobstructed, joyful eloquence.

A talk given on August 21, 1983,
at the City of Ten Thousand Buddhas

見賢思齊英勇士

賢人的一舉一動，一言一行，
堪作為我們的模範。

今天對聯的題目是：「見賢思齊英勇士」。我們要
效法賢人，他們所行所作，皆為榜樣。

什麼是賢人？就是賢而有德的人。見到賢人，一定
向他看齊，向他學習，要和他一樣有道德，有風度
，有學識，有涵養。但這並不是想一想就算了，而
是要認真去實踐，努力學習。賢人的一舉一動，一
言一行，堪作為我們的模範；若不學習，只是在想
，是沒有用處。你能認真去學習，才是英勇之士，
也是大英雄，也是大法師。

英勇之士，不是草包。什麼是「草包」？簡單地說

A Hero Is One Who Strives to Emulate Worthy People

Every word and deed of the worthies is a good example for us.

The topic for today's matching couplets is: "A hero is one who sees worthy ones and strives to be like them." We should take worthy people as our models and emulate their conduct.

Who are the worthy ones? They are people with virtue and talent. When we meet worthy people, we should learn from them and strive to be as virtuous, refined, learned, and cultured as they are. We shouldn't just think about it; we should work hard and really try to emulate them. Their every word and deed is a good example for us. But if we only think about their example without trying to emulate it, it won't be of any use. Only through diligent study can we be a great hero, a great Dharma Master.

A hero is not a simpleton or a fool. Someone may say, "Well,

，就是愚笨的人。有人說：「他是個鹹（賢）人呀
！活該是鹹人，與我沒有關係。他要做鹹人，我要
做淡人。」這種淡而無味的人，不管好，不管壞，
一切無所謂，反正混吃等死，死了就算了，這是懶
惰人的思想，永遠沒出息。

一九八三年八月十三日
開示於萬佛聖城無言堂

he may be a salty [pronounced the same as "worthy" in Chinese] person, but that's got nothing to do with it. If he's a salty person, I want to be a bland person." This kind of a bland and flavorless person doesn't care about anything; he just eats his food and waits to die, thinking, "After I die, I can forget about everything!" That is the attitude of a lazy, good-for-nothing bum.

A talk given on August 13, 1983,
in the Hall of No Words at the City of Ten Thousand Buddhas

萬佛聖城六大宗旨

不向外邊粉刷，
而把內邊莊嚴清淨。

遠來的朋友，近來的善知識，我們大家共同來研究
做人成佛的道理。我們做人，一定要本著「孝、悌
、忠、信、禮、義、廉、恥」八德為標準。要想成
佛，將這八德的範圍擴大，孝於全世界，悌於全世
界，忠於全世界，信於全世界，乃至仁義禮智於全
世界，推而廣之，擴而充之，大而無外，小而無內
，用這種精神，去行佛法；可是這種精神，不容易
做到盡善盡美的程度。

現在一般修行人，覺得修持佛法，好像丟了什麼似
的。為什麼說丟了什麼似的？因為沒有什麼利益可

106

The Six Guidelines of the City of Ten Thousand Buddhas

We don't decorate the outside; instead we adorn and purify the inside.

Friends from afar and good advisors from nearby, let us investigate together the principles of being a person and becoming a Buddha. In being a person, we should take the eight virtues-filial piety, brotherhood, loyalty, trustworthiness, propriety, righteousness, incorruptibility, and a sense of shame-as our standard. To become a Buddha, we should extend the scope of the eight virtues and be filial, dutiful, loyal, trustworthy, kind, just, proper, and wise towards the whole world. We should keep expanding these qualities until they are so vast there's nothing beyond them, yet so minute there's nothing inside them. That is the kind of spirit we should have in practicing Buddhism, but it is not easy to perfect.

Nowadays some cultivators feel as if they have lost some-

取，沒有利益可得，就好像吃了虧，故無精打采，
對修持不起勁。善知識請注意：

> 捨不了死，換不了生；
> 捨不了假，成不了真。

我們把眼光放大，把思想放寬，不要只知道有我自
己，或者只知道有我的家庭，或者只知道有我的國
家，要將心量擴大到盡虛空遍法界，要為全人類的
利益著想，不要只為自己打算。

對人類有利益，而不傷害人類，那就是修行佛道的
基本條件。怎樣利益人類，怎樣不傷害人類？就是
實行萬佛聖城六大宗旨：

第一「不爭」。我們不和任何人爭；你和我爭，我
不和你爭，你罵我，我不罵你。你打我，我不打你
，你欺負我，我不欺負你；這是萬佛聖城一貫的宗
旨。

釋迦牟尼佛在往昔為忍辱仙人時，就不和歌利王爭

thing when they practice Buddhism. Because they don't obtain any apparent benefit, they feel they are suffering a loss. And so they lose their enthusiasm for cultivation. Good advisors, please be aware that:

If you don't renounce death,
You can't exchange it for life;
If you don't give up the false,
You can't achieve the true.

We should broaden our views, expand our thinking, and not be concerned solely with ourselves and our own families and countries. We should expand our minds to encompass the universe. We should think about helping all of humanity, instead of just making plans for ourselves.

Benefiting people and not harming them is a basic requirement of cultivating the Buddha Way. How can we benefit and not harm people? By practicing the Six Guidelines of the City of Ten Thousand Buddhas:

1. *Not fighting.* We don't fight with anyone. You may fight with me, but I won't fight with you; you may scold me, but I won't scold you; you may beat me, but I won't beat you; you may bully me, but I won't bully you. That is the overall principle at the City of Ten Thousand Buddhas.

When Shakyamuni Buddha was an immortal cultivating patience in a past life, he did not fight with King Kali;

，以德來感化。歌利王割截他的四肢，反問他有沒有瞋恨心？忍辱仙人説：「沒有。」歌利王不相信，又問：「有什麼可以證明你沒有瞋恨心？」

忍辱仙人説：「我要是沒有瞋恨心，我的四肢，立即重生。」説完之後，果然四肢重新生出，恢復原狀。忍辱仙人不但不生瞋恨之心，反而生出大悲心，乃對歌利王説：「我將來成佛，第一個先度你出家修道。」

後來忍辱仙人成佛，就是釋迦牟尼佛，他本著往昔的願力，到鹿野苑，度憍陳如尊者（歌利王的後身）出家，爲五比丘之一。

第二「不貪」。貪心一起，就貪而無厭，無論是金錢，或是物質，總覺得不夠，愈貪愈不夠，愈不夠愈貪，貪到老了，還不覺悟。被「貪」字害了一輩子，到死的時候，還覺得哪件事或者哪個東西還沒有得到手，深表遺憾，這是多麼可憐！萬佛聖城第二大宗旨，不貪任何的金錢、利益，或好名。總之，一切不貪，各安本分弘揚佛法，續佛慧命。

instead, he taught and transformed him with virtue. King Kali cut off the immortal's four limbs and asked him if he was angry. The patient immortal said, "No." King Kali didn't believe him and asked him to prove it. The immortal said, "If I have no anger, my limbs will grow back." After he said that, his limbs were restored. Instead of being angry with the king, the immortal made a compassionate promise to the king, saying, "When I become a Buddha, you will be the first one I come to save, and you will renounce the householder's life and cultivate." Later, when the immortal became Shakyamuni Buddha, in accord with his vow he went to the Deer Park to teach the Venerable Ajnata-kaundinya (King Kali in a previous life), who renounced the householder's life and became one of the first five Bhikshus.

2. Not being greedy. Once greed arises, it is insatiable. Whether you crave money or material things, you are never satisfied. The greedier you become, the less satisfied you are; the less satisfied you are, the greedier you become. You will be greedy until you grow old, and you still won't understand. Greed may have ruined your whole life, but in the end you still express deep regret for not having obtained certain things. How pitiful! The City's second guideline is not to be greedy for money, benefit, or fame; not to be greedy for anything. We just do our basic duty and propagate the Buddhadharma in order to continue the Buddha's wisdom life.

佛在世時，有一天佛和阿難尊者，在路上遇見一堆黃金，佛看也不看便走過去，阿難尊者的定力未到火候，還要看一眼才走過去。佛對阿難說：「那是毒蛇。」

這時候，在田地耕種的農人，一聽到毒蛇，就去看看，啊！原來是黃金，於是歡天喜地拿回家中，頓時成為暴發戶。鄰居懷疑農人的錢來路不明，於是向國王報告。國王派人將農人捉來，問他錢的來源，他據實說，國王又派人到他家檢查，發現有很多金子，全部拿回來，呈獻給國王。國王一見，大發雷霆，原來這些黃金，都是國庫丟的黃金，於是認為農人是強盜，就把他關在監獄中。這時候，農人才知道佛說是毒蛇的真理。由此可證，意外之財不可貪。

第三「不求」。萬佛聖城的宗旨——不攀緣、不求緣、不化緣。這個「求」字和「貪」字差不多。「貪」是若有若無；「求」是實際的企求，到處去拉攏關係，不擇手段地求，求什麼？求金錢，求物質

When the Buddha was in the world, one day he and the Venerable Ananda came upon a pile of gold. The Buddha walked past the pile without even glancing at it. The Venerable Ananda had not perfected his samadhi, so walking by he took a glance at it. The Buddha told him, "That's a poisonous snake." Meanwhile, a farmer tilling his field overheard the mention of a poisonous snake and went to take a look, only to discover that it was actually a pile of gold. Overjoyed, he took the gold home and instantly became a rich man. But his neighbor was suspicious of the source of his wealth, and reported it to the king. The king sent for the farmer and asked him where he had gotten the money from. The farmer truthfully told his story. The king then sent his people to search the farmer's house, and they found lots of gold. They took the gold back and showed it to the king. Seeing the gold, the king became furious, because it was stolen from the state treasury. The king thought the farmer had stolen it and threw him in jail. Only then did the farmer understand the truth behind the Buddha's having called the gold a poisonous snake. The above story illustrates that one shouldn't be greedy for unexpected wealth.

3. Not seeking. The principle of the City is not to exploit, beg, or seek. Seeking is similar to being greedy. Greed is something intangible and hard to pin down. Seeking is the actual pursuit of something through exploiting social connections, trying to get it by hook or by crook. What kinds of things do we seek? We seek money, material things, and all kinds of

。總而言之，求一切利益。萬佛聖城是向內求，不向外求。內求於心，把癡心妄想、狂心野性、妒忌障礙、貪瞋癡等，掃除乾淨。不向外邊粉刷，而把內邊莊嚴清淨。有人說：「肚裏根本就是邋遢，無論怎麼清理，還是邋遢。」這是表面的邋遢；但我們的自性清淨，沒有染污。

所謂：

人到無求品自高。

不求於人，品格自然清高，沒有邋遢的思想。

佛在世時，有一對窮夫婦，不但無立錐之地，也無隔宿之糧。住在山洞中，夫婦倆人只有一條褲子，誰外出乞食，誰就穿這條褲子，他們窮的程度，不問而知。有一天，來了一位辟支佛，試探他們有沒有貪求心，於是向他們化緣。夫婦倆人商量如何供養這位出家人？實在無物可供養，乃將唯有一條褲子供養，但是沒有任何所求，只是本著一顆至誠的心來供養出家人。

benefits. But at the City of Ten Thousand Buddhas the seeking is directed inward, not outward. Seeking within our minds, we sweep out the foolish thoughts, the mad mind and wild nature, jealousy, obstruction, greed, anger, stupidity, and so forth. We don't decorate the outside; instead we adorn and purify the inside. Someone may say, "It's filthy inside. No matter how much you sweep, it's still filthy." But the filth is only superficial. Our inherent nature is pure and clean, without defilement. It is said,

> When people reach the state of not seeking,
> Their character will naturally be noble.

If you don't seek anything from anyone, your character will naturally be noble and free of impure thoughts.

When the Buddha was in the world, there was a poor couple that had neither a place to stay nor food for the next day. They lived in a cave and their only possession was a pair of pants. Whoever went out to beg would wear the pants. That's how poor they were. One day a Pratyekabuddha came to test them to see if they had greedy minds. He begged for alms at their cave. The couple discussed how they could make offerings to this monk. They really couldn't find anything, so with a sincere mind they offered the pants to the Pratyekabuddha and sought nothing in return.

115

這位辟支佛遂將褲子供養佛。釋迦牟尼佛知道這條褲的來龍去脈，當著法會大眾宣佈這條褲子的來源，讚揚布施褲子的施主，有如何的功德。當時國王也在座，聞此消息，覺得慚愧——在自己的國家內，還有這樣的窮人！於是就派一位大臣，送給這對夫婦很多的飲食及衣服，給他們房子住，給他們工作。此時夫婦因無求之念，而得如此之報，所謂「捨一得萬報」。

第四「不自私」。世界為什麼壞到這種程度？都因為人人太自私。對自己有利益的事，便爭先恐後去做；要是對自己沒有利益，就袖手旁觀，或者以隔岸觀火的心情來說風涼話。

自私有多種，對於地位自私，對於名譽自私，對於權利自私，對於金錢自私。一言以蔽之，一切的一切都因為自私在作怪。所以不管他人，只顧自己。

所謂：

　　　摩訶薩不管他，彌陀佛各顧各。

116

The Pratyekabuddha took the pants and offered them to the Buddha. Shakyamuni Buddha knew the story behind the pants, and related it to the Dharma assembly. He praised the donors for the merit and virtue they had created. The king of the country, who happened to be present, heard the story and felt ashamed that there should be such poor people in his own country. Thereupon he sent an official with lots of food and clothing for that couple, and provided them with housing and employment. Because that couple didn't have thoughts of seeking, they got such a reward. That is known as "giving something and being rewarded ten thousand times over."

4. *Not being selfish.* Why is this world deteriorating at such a rate? It's all because people are too selfish. When it comes to things for their own benefit, they strive to be first. But as for things that don't benefit them, they stand aside and watch, perhaps making facetious remarks with an attitude of "watching a fire from a safe distance."

There are many kinds of selfishness. Some people are selfish regarding position, others about reputation, power, or money. In general, it is selfishness at work when people care only for themselves and disregard others. As the saying goes,

> Mahasattva, don't pay attention to others;
> Amitabha, it's every man for himself.

這是小乘的思想。儒家也曾說過：

> 各人自掃門前雪，莫管他人瓦上霜。

這是不管閒事的作風。人生存在這個世界，就要互相幫忙、互相援助。所以應提倡大乘思想，學習菩薩精神，聞苦救難，不可有幸災樂禍的心理。

世人要是沒有自私心，便能和任何人和睦相處，如同一家人。因為有自私心，才弄出很多的問題。所以不自私是萬佛聖城第四大宗旨。

第五「不自利」。這個宗旨比第四個宗旨「不自私」，更為重要。誰也不願意不自利；可是一定要這樣「不自利」，世界才能好。不自利就是要利益他人，把自己忘了，所謂「捨己為人」，這種精神超過菩薩的行為。菩薩是自利利他，自度度他，自覺覺他。我們不自利，只是利他，只是度他，只是覺他。

第六「不妄語」。就是不存心騙人；人為什麼打妄

This is the way of thinking of the Small Vehicle. There is a saying in the Confucian school: "Sweep the snow in front of your own door, and don't be concerned with the frost on others' roof tiles." That is the attitude of not meddling in other people's affairs. But people in this world should help and support one another. That's why we should promote the thinking of the Great Vehicle and learn the spirit of the Bodhisattvas, who rescue those in distress upon hearing their cries of suffering. We shouldn't gloat over others' misfortunes.

If people in this world weren't selfish, we could all get along harmoniously like one family. Selfishness creates a lot of problems. So not being selfish is the fourth guideline of the City of Ten Thousand Buddhas.

5. *Not pursuing personal advantage.* This principle is even more important than the fourth one. No one is willing to give up personal gain. But if the world is to be wholesome, it has to be this way. No pursuit of personal advantage means benefitting others and forgetting oneself, "forsaking oneself for the sake of others." This attitude surpasses the Bodhisattvas' conduct. Bodhisattvas benefit themselves and others, save themselves and others, and enlighten themselves and others. But we benefit only others, not ourselves; we save only others, and help only others to become enlightened.

6. *Not lying.* This means having no intention to deceive

語呢？因為他怕自己的利益失去，怕吃虧，所以他才撒謊。要是常常用真心待人，則自然就遵守不妄語的宗旨。

這六大宗旨，一般人聽來很不高興、很不受用。無論誰不高興、誰不受用，我不管，我要和大家說明白。我從來不反對世界任何的事情，為什麼？因為我的宗旨，一切 Okay!（好！）可是有人反對我，那我最歡迎，絕不反駁。今天簡單將萬佛聖城六大宗旨向各位介紹。如果詳細來講，說不能盡，終身行之，受用匪淺。

一九八三年八月十四日
開示於萬佛聖城

120

people. Why do people lie? Because they are afraid of losing their advantage, afraid of taking a loss. If we can treat people with sincerity, we will naturally uphold the sixth guideline of not lying.

Some people may not be happy to hear the Six Guidelines, and they may feel very uncomfortable. I don't care if people are unhappy or ill at ease; I just want to make this clear to all of you. I never oppose anything in this world. Why not? Because my motto is: "Everything is okay." However, if people oppose me, they are most welcome to, since I won't argue. Today, I have briefly introduced the Six Guidelines of the City to you. If I spoke in detail, you wouldn't hear the end of it. You can practice them throughout your whole life; they are immensely useful.

A talk given on August 14, 1983,
at the Buddha Hall, the City of Ten Thousand Buddhas

修行人不可攀緣

與人結好，私自贈送，
這種行為是破壞道場的規矩。

我的宗旨：

　　凍死不攀緣，
　　餓死不化緣，窮死不求緣，
　　隨緣不變，不變隨緣，
　　抱定我們三大宗旨；
　　捨命為佛事，
　　造命為本事，正命為僧事，
　　即事明理，明理即事，
　　推行祖師一脈心傳。

這是我們的本份，盼共勉之。

Cultivators Must Not Exploit Conditions

To befriend people and give them private gifts violates the monastic rules.

My creed is:

> Freezing, we do not scheme;
> Starving, we do not beg;
> Dying of poverty, we ask for nothing.
> We accord with conditions, but never waver;
> We remain steadfast, yet accord with every situation.
> These are our three great principles:
> We dedicate our lives to do the Buddha's work,
> We forge our lives as our basic duty,
> We rectify our lives to fulfill the Sangha's role.
> We express our ideals within our daily affairs,
> So that within our daily affairs our ideals shine forth.
> Thus we continue unbroken
> > the legacy of the Patriarch's mind.

This is our basic duty, and I hope we can encourage each other.

修行人，不要有攀緣心，要有不貪不染的清淨心。我常對你們講，凡是出家修行，一心求道，什麼也不要，什麼也不貪。就是一棵草，也不能隨便送給人，也不能隨便向人索取，所謂：

一芥不以與人，
一芥不以取諸人。

對於「緣」，要分得清清楚楚。要清淨這個「緣」，不要污染這個「緣」。清淨緣，是沒有貪心；染污緣，是有貪心。出家人可以受供養，但不可貪供養；不貪圖供養，才是真正佛的弟子。

你本來應該接受供養，可是你不受，這才是有志氣。諸位不是爲衣食而出家，穿好衣服，吃好東西，而不好好修行，那有何用？凡是身外之物，應看成平常，不要看得那樣重，所謂「君子謀道不謀食」，今改爲「君子謀道不謀衣」，對於好食物不要貪求，能吃飽就算了，對於好衣服不要貪求，能蔽寒就算了。

Cultivators should not exploit conditions. Instead, you should have clear, pure minds that aren't greedy or defiled. As I always tell you, people who have entered the monastic life to cultivate should seek the Way single-mindedly, wanting nothing else and being greedy for nothing. You can't carelessly give even a mustard seed to other people, nor can you ask people for one. There is an idiom:

Don't casually give away a mustard seed;
Don't casually accept a mustard seed from anyone.

You should have a very clear understanding of affinities. You want to purify your affinities and not pollute them. Lack of greed makes an affinity pure. Greed pollutes an affinity. Monks and nuns may accept offerings, but they should not be greedy for them. A person who does not crave offerings is a true disciple of the Buddha.

To decline offerings that you are entitled to accept shows resolute integrity. You didn't enter the monastic life for the sake of food or clothes. If you wear fine clothes and eat well, but don't cultivate, what good is that? As for things that are not essential, we should treat them in an ordinary way and not put too much emphasis on them. There is a saying: "A superior person seeks the Way, not food." Today I will change it to: "A superior person seeks the Way, not clothing." Don't be greedy for good food; you should be content if you can eat your fill; don't be greedy for nice clothes; just make sure you wear enough to protect you from the cold.

古人說：

> 君子安貧；達人知命。

出家人，要知道在道業沒有成就之前，不可欠債。要是欠債，會把你繞住，不得解脫。尤其是這些不清淨的緣，害你拔不出腿來，得不到自在。可是一般出家人，歡喜受人供養，接受人的果儀。被不清淨的緣縛住，就不容易超出三界。染污緣的繩子，把你綑繞得緊緊，無法解脫。所以，不要貪戀這種不真實的東西，免得麻煩。

出家人分為七等——

（一）頭等出家人：一身輕飄飄，什麼也沒有，一塵不染，萬緣皆空。

（二）二等出家人：手持布袋；袋中有什麼，外人不會知道。

（三）三等出家人：肩挑擔子；因為放不下，把所有的家當，走到哪裏，挑到哪裏，雖然是重擔（約

The ancients said,

> A superior person feels at ease in poverty;
> A wise person understands the will of Heaven.

Monks and nuns should be aware that until one accomplishes the Way, one cannot incur debts. If you have debts, they will bind you and hinder your liberation. Impure affinities in particular will trap you so that you can't be free. Ordinary monks and nuns, however, like to receive offerings and get bound by impure affinities. If you do so, it won't be easy to transcend the Three Realms. The rope of polluted affinities will bind you so tightly that you won't be able to get free. Don't indulge in these unreal things, and then you won't have any trouble.

Monastics who have renounced the life of a householder can be grouped into seven categories.

1. Monastics of the first rank have no burdens. They are not polluted by any dust; all their affinities are emptied.

2. Monastics who rank second hold cloth bags in their hands, and no one knows what's in them.

3. Monastics of the third rank carry their loads with poles on their shoulders; it's everything they have. It's a heavy load (about a hundred pounds), but since they cannot renounce everything yet, they are willing to carry this load

有一百磅），也甘願挑之。在美國這個國家，沒有擔子，而用背袋，是大同小異的意思。

（四）四等出家人：東西用汽車裝。

（五）五等出家人：東西用火車裝。

（六）六等出家人：東西用輪船裝。

（七）七等出家人：東西用飛機裝。

這是出家人所犯的通病。

我希望你們跟著我出家，早成佛道；不能成佛，也要作菩薩。總之，要利益他人，不要利益自己。不可將常住的東西隨便送人情，你認為有功德，其實是盜僧伽物，與人結好，私自贈送，這種行為，是破壞道場的規矩。有這種行為就要趕快糾正過來，不可再犯；沒有這種行為，謹之！慎之！

一九八三年八月十五日
開示於萬佛聖城

wherever they go. (In this country people use backpacks instead of carrying poles, but it's about the same.)

4. Monastics of the fourth rank use cars to haul their belongings.

5. Monastics of the fifth rank use trains.

6. Monastics of the sixth rank use ships.

7. Monastics of the seventh rank use airplanes.

Having too much stuff is a common fault among monastics.

I allowed you to join the monastic life, and I hope you will become Buddhas soon. If you cannot become Buddhas, you should become Bodhisattvas. In any case, you should benefit others, not yourselves. Don't casually give away the temple's possessions for the sake of establishing relationships. You may think you're creating merit and virtue, but actually you are stealing from the Sangha. To befriend people and give them private gifts violates the monastic rules. If you have done so, correct your behavior quickly and don't ever do it again. Be careful about such things.

A talk given on August 15, 1983,
at the City of Ten Thousand Buddhas

開五眼才見真龍

你想知道嗎？趕快用功修道，
專心打坐，少打妄想，不要發脾氣。

「龍」究竟是什麼樣子？一般人是不知道的。除非
開五眼的聖人才知道龍的真面目。不過，中國人所
畫的龍，頭上有角，身上有鱗，眼睛突出，嘴巴很
大，有鬍鬚，有四足，身很長，尾很短。畫龍的人
，只畫龍頭不畫龍尾，所謂「神龍見首不見尾」，
表示有神祕之感。

中國人繪龍為什麼是這樣子？因為曾經有位禪師，
他在定中所見龍的形相是這樣子。龍有神通，變化
莫測，能大能小，能隱能現。六祖大師曾經用缽將
巨龍降伏，為南華寺除害。

Open the Five Eyes and See the Real Dragons

Do you want to know? Well, hurry up and work hard, concentrate in meditation, cut down your false thoughts, and don't become angry.

What do dragons look like? Ordinary people don't know. Only sages who have opened the five eyes know what dragons really look like. The dragons depicted by Chinese artists have horns, scales, prominent eyes, a large mouth, whiskers, four feet, a long body and a short tail. The artists paint only the dragon's head and not its tail. The saying, "You can see only a divine dragon's head, not its tail" refers to the sense of mystery here.

Why did the Chinese paint dragons that way? Because there was a Dhyana Master who saw a dragon in his samadhi that looked like that. Dragons have spiritual penetrations. Their transformations are inconceivable. They can become big or small; visible or invisible. The Sixth Patriarch used his bowl to subdue a giant dragon that had been a menace to Nanhua Monastery.

龍是一條大蟲，因爲往昔修行時，乘急，所以有神通；戒緩，所以墮爲畜生。

龍的種類不同，有金龍、白龍、青龍、黑龍，有胎生的龍，有卵生的龍，有濕生的龍，有化生的龍，又有虯龍、鷹龍、蛟龍、驪龍，又有天龍、地龍、王龍、人龍，又有魚化龍、馬化龍、象化龍、蛤蟆化龍。

龍有四種苦：

（一）被大鵬金翅鳥所吞苦。
（二）交尾變蛇形苦。
（三）小蟲咬身苦。
（四）熱沙燙身苦。

龍的職業是佈雲降雨。可是有五種情形不能降雨：

（一）火大增盛。
（二）風吹雲散。
（三）阿修羅收雲入海。

Dragons are giant worms. In their past cultivation, since they diligently cultivated the Great Vehicle, they are endowed with supernatural powers. However, since they were lax in holding the precepts, they have fallen into the animal realm. There are different varieties of dragons, such as gold, white, blue, and black dragons. Some dragons are born from embryos, some from eggs, some from moisture, and others by transformation. There are also two-horned young dragons, eagle dragons, single-horned dragons, black dragons, celestial dragons, earthly dragons, imperial dragons, human dragons, fish-transformed dragons, horse-transformed dragons, elephant-transformed dragons, and toad-transformed dragons. Dragons undergo four sufferings:

(1) the suffering of being swallowed by golden-winged *peng* birds,
(2) the suffering of tails intersecting and being changed to snake form,
(3) the suffering of being bitten by insects, and
(4) the suffering of being scorched by hot sands.

The dragons' duty is to spread clouds and make the rain fall. But there are five situations under which they cannot make rain:

(1) the fire element is in preponderance,
(2) the wind blows the clouds asunder,
(3) *asuras* condense the clouds into the sea,

（四）雨師放逸。

（五）眾生尊重。

各位想知道龍的形狀？那麼，就努力修行用功打坐，開了五眼，便見到眞龍的本來面目。我現在講「龍的公案」，這是我親身經驗的故事，千眞萬確，絕非杜撰。

我在東北的時候，收了一個徒弟，法名果舜，他很用功修行，不到半年的時間，打坐能入定，在定中能知道因果循環報應的道理，修持功夫頗到家。後來他自己到外邊建一所茅棚，作爲修行的道場。落成之日，請我去開光，我領四個徒弟前去，其中有兩個徒弟已開五眼。當時我沒有注意在茅棚的旁邊有龍王廟，當天的境界來了，我們正在打坐的時候，那兩個開五眼的徒弟來到我面前說：「師父！茅棚外邊來了十條龍，要皈依師父。」

我對徒弟說：「你不要胡說，你怎麼知道他們是龍？他們皈依我做什麼？我怎能作他們的師父？我沒有他們那樣大的本領。」

(4) the rainmakers are remiss, or

(5) living beings' offenses are heavy.

Do you want to know the dragons' real form? Then you must apply effort in cultivation and work hard in meditation, and after you open your five eyes you will be able to see the original face of the dragon. Now let me tell you a story about dragons. This is my personal experience. It is absolutely true and not made up.

When I was in Manchuria, I accepted a disciple named Guo Shun. He worked very hard in cultivation. In less than half a year he could enter samadhi when he sat in meditation. When he was in samadhi, he learned the principle of cause and effect and its resultant retributions. His skill in cultivation was quite good. Later on he went out to build a hut as his Way-place for cultivation. On the day of its inauguration, he invited me over to perform the opening ceremonies. I brought along four disciples, two of whom had opened the five eyes. I did not notice there was a dragon temple next to the hut. The state came that day. While we were sitting in meditation, the two disciples who had opened the five eyes came to me and said, "Master! There are ten dragons outside the hut. They want to take refuge with you."

I said, "Don't talk nonsense! How do you know they are dragons? What do they want to take refuge with me for? How could I be their master? I don't have any great ability like they do."

徒弟説：「他們自己説是龍，現在跪在外邊，一定要求皈依。」

當時正逢初夏，天旱無雨，田地的禾苗，差不多枯死。我對龍（化人身）説：「你們皈依我可以，但是我有一個條件。你們是龍，專管下雨，現在哈爾濱附近很久沒有下雨，非常乾旱，明天如果下雨，那麼，後天就給你們授皈依；要是不下雨，就不收你們作弟子。」

眾龍異口同聲地説：「我們的職責就是行雨，可是沒有玉皇大帝的敕令，我們不敢下雨，否則，要受處分。」

我又説：「你們到玉皇大帝座前對他説：『哈爾濱有位出家人，請求在哈爾濱四周四十里之內降雨。』這是我的條件。」

第二天果然天降大雨，解除旱災，在哈爾濱四十里以內，普降甘霖。第三天，便給這十條龍授皈依，共同法名叫「急修」。他們皈依之後，隱形不見，

The disciples said, "They themselves said they were dragons. They are kneeling outside now, insisting on taking refuge."

This happened in the early summer. There hadn't been any rain. The young grain shoots in the fields were almost withered. I told the dragons (who had assumed human form), "You can take refuge with me on one condition. You are dragons and you are in charge of rainfall. Now there hasn't been any rain in the vicinity of Harbin. It is very dry. If it rains tomorrow, I'll transmit the Three Refuges to you the day after. However, if there's no rain, I won't take you as my disciples."

The dragons said in unison, "Our duty is to make the rain fall. But we don't dare make rain without orders from the Jade Emperor; otherwise we'll be punished."

I said, "You go before the Jade Emperor and tell him that there is a monk in Harbin asking for rain within a radius of forty *li* [13.3 American miles] from Harbin. Those are my terms."

On the second day it rained and the drought was over. Sweet dew fell within the area forty *li* around Harbin. On the third day, I transmitted the Three Refuges to the ten dragons and gave them a collective Dharma name, "Quickly Cultivate." After the refuge ceremony they disappeared and went back to teach and transform their own

去度化同類的龍。從此之後，我無論到什麼地方，都有水用。我在香港，香港有水用；我到萬佛聖城，萬佛聖城有水用。這不是奇蹟出現，乃是因為十條龍及其眷屬都來護法的緣故。

有人問：「師父！你看那十條龍是什麼樣子？」皈依我的龍，乃變化人的形相，和普通人一樣，沒有什麼區別。開五眼的人知道是龍。你想知道嗎？趕快用功修道，專心打坐，少打妄想，不要發脾氣，無論是逆境或順境都要忍耐，不可起貪心，到一念不生一塵不染的境界，自然開五眼。那時候，你就能清清楚楚看見龍是什麼樣子！

kind. From then on, wherever I went I could get water. When I was in Hong Kong, Hong Kong had water. I came to the City of Ten Thousand Buddhas, and the City has water. That is not a miracle. It happens because the ten dragons and their families have all come to protect the Dharma.

Someone asked, "Master, what did the ten dragons look like?" The dragons that took refuge with me had changed themselves into human form. They looked no different from ordinary people. People who have opened the five eyes would know they were dragons. Do you want to know? Then hurry up and work hard, concentrate in meditation, cut down your false thoughts, don't become angry, be patient with both good and bad states, and don't be greedy. When you reach the state where not one thought arises and the mind is totally pristine, you will naturally open the five eyes. Then you can see clearly what dragons look like!

人生如夢要清醒

來，從什麼地方來的？
去，往什麼地方去呢？

人來到這個世界，把真的放下，拿起假的，所以生生世世背覺合塵，醉生夢死。醉生就是在生的時候，好像喝醉酒似的，不知怎樣生來；夢死就是在死的時候，好像在作夢似的，不知怎樣死去。人人皆在夢中，不知何日能清醒，所謂「人生如夢」，以假為真，為名為利，貪無止境。

你在夢中，又升官，又發財，又有地位，又有名譽，嬌妻美妾，兒孫滿堂，榮華富貴，享受不盡。假設這時，在夢中有人對你說：「這都是虛妄的，不是真實的。」你絕對不會相信。等你的甜蜜夢清醒

Life Is Like a Dream: Wake Up!

Where do we come from when we arrive?
Where do we go to when we leave?

When people come into this world, they put down the real and pick up the unreal. That is why in life after life we turn against enlightenment, unite with the dust, and muddle our way through life as if drunk or in a dream. When we are born, we seem to be drunk and unaware of how we got born; when we die, we seem to be in a dream, unaware of how we die. People are all dreaming, and there's no knowing when they will wake up. It's said that life is like a dream. We take the false for the real, and become insatiably greedy for fame and profit.

In your dream, you are promoted and become wealthy; you have high social status, a good reputation, a beautiful wife, lovely mistresses, and a house full of children and grandchildren; you enjoy boundless affluence, wealth and honor. If at some time during the dream someone were to tell you,

時，沒有人告訴你這是作夢，你自己也知道原來是在作夢哪！

你昨夜在夢中，讀書中狀元，當了宰相，作了皇帝，成了神仙，其樂無窮。今天早晨醒了，啊！原是一場夢呀！這是清醒了；如果沒有醒，認為是真的，就貪戀不捨，不肯放下，執迷不悟。

我們現在就是在作白日夢，沒有清醒，所以糊塗而來，糊塗而去。來，從什麼地方來的？去，往什麼地方去呢？不知道；一輩子也沒有清醒。各位想想看！這有什麼意義？有什麼可留戀？有什麼值得放不下呢？

我們一生被「三毒」及「五欲」的繩子綑得結結實實，連轉身的自由都沒有，更談不到解脫。所以發心出家修道，用功打坐，努力拜佛，就是解三毒和五欲的繩子，終有一天，能完全解開。那時候就清醒了，回頭一看，過去所作所為，完全如夢，一切不如法。現在清醒了，便能出離三界，不受生死的

"These things are all unreal," you would never believe that person. However, after you woke up from your sweet dream, even if no one told you it was a dream, you would know that you'd been dreaming.

Last night in a dream, you came out first in the imperial examinations, got appointed prime minister, later became emperor, and finally became an immortal enjoying boundless happiness. This morning you wake up¢w"Oh! It was a spring dream!" That is when you are awake. If you don't wake up and you continue to think it's real, then you become enamored of it and can't let go. Unable to let go, you become deeply attached and deluded. Right now we are daydreaming, not awake. So we come into this world muddled and leave muddled. Where do we come from when we arrive? Where do we go when we leave? We don't know. During our whole life long, we are never once awake. Think about it: Is that meaningful? What do we want to stay around for? What is so precious that we cannot bear to put it down?

In our lives, we are tightly bound by the ropes of the three poisons and the five desires. We don't even have the freedom to turn around, let alone be liberated. Hence, we must resolve to enter the monastic life and cultivate the Way, meditating and bowing to the Buddha with vigor. Those are the ways to untie the ropes of the three poisons and the five desires. The day will come when the ropes are completely untied. At that time, you will be awake. Looking back on what you have done, you will find that it was completely

限制，生死自由，願生即生，願死即死，這種境界，遂心如意，來去自由，才是眞正解脫，所謂「大夢初醒」。

我們現在把假的抓住，把眞的忘了。什麼是假的？財色名食睡這五欲的快樂是假的。什麼是眞的？涅槃四德——「常樂我淨」的快樂是眞的。可是奇怪的人類，眞的丟了也不怕，把假的丟了卻起恐怖。爲什麼？因爲認賊作子，捨本逐末，以假爲眞，沒有清醒，還在夢中，貪戀夢中的境界。

我們因爲起惑造業受報的緣故，好像一粒微塵，在空中飄上飄下，做不得主，隨著業力在六道輪迴中轉來轉去。所謂「打不破名利關，跳不出輪迴圈」，什麼時候不爲名利境界所轉，那時就脫離六道輪迴的樊籠。

一九八三年八月二十一日
開示於萬佛聖城

like a dream, and nothing you did was in accord with the Dharma. Since you now are fully awake, you can leave the Three Realms and not be bound by birth and death. You will have control over your own birth and death: you can be born if you like to and die when you want to. This state, where everything is just as you wish, where you can come and go freely, is true liberation. It is like waking up from a big dream.

But now we hold on to what's false and forget about what's true. What is false? The objects of the five desires: wealth, sex, fame, food and sleep. What is true? The happiness of the four virtues of Nirvana-permanence, bliss, true self, and purity. And yet we human beings are so strange: We're not afraid of losing what's true, but we're terrified when what's false is lost. Why is that? Because we take a thief for our son, we reject the roots in favor of the twigs, take the false for the true, and are continually dreaming, hooked by dream states.

Because of delusion, we create karma and then receive the retribution. We are like a dust mote floating up and down in the air, led by the power of our karma, revolving in the six paths, with no control of our own. It is said, "If you can't clear the hurdles of fame and profit, you won't be able to leap out of the cycle of rebirth." When fame and benefit cease to attract you, you'll escape the trap of rebirth in the six paths.

A talk given on August 21, 1983,
at the City of Ten Thousand Buddhas

何謂五衰相現

等到天福享盡時，
仍然墮落在輪迴中，接受應受的果報。

善事做多了，善功德具足了，就生到天上，享受天上的快樂。天人時時在定中，得到禪悅爲食，法喜充滿的快樂。但這不究竟，等到天福享盡時，仍然墮落在輪迴中，接受應受的果報。

天人的福報，思衣衣至，思食食來；衣服只有三銖重（二十四銖爲一兩），所謂「天衣無縫」，不需要裁縫，大小正合體，不肥不瘦，恰到好處。一想吃東西，食物即刻現前，其量不多不少，令食者滿意。

What Are the Five Signs of Decay of the Gods?

When they exhaust their celestial blessings, they must re-enter the transmigratory cycle to receive the retribution they deserve.

If we do many good deeds and achieve wholesome merit and virtue, we can be reborn in the heavens to enjoy celestial happiness. Celestial beings are always in samadhi. They "take Dhyana bliss as their food and are filled with the joy of Dharma." However, their state is not an ultimate one. When they exhaust their celestial blessings, they must re-enter the transmigratory cycle to receive the retribution they deserve.

The gods are so blessed that clothing or food materializes as soon as they think of them. Their clothing is extremely lightweight; hence the saying, "Celestial clothes are seamless." They don't need tailors. Their clothes are always just the right size, not too big, not too small. When celestial beings wish to eat, food instantly appears, in exactly the right amount to satisfy the eater.

天人臨終時，便有五種衰象：

（一）花冠枯萎：天人所戴的花冠，非常莊嚴，永不凋謝。臨終時，花冠自然枯萎 。

（二）衣服垢膩：天人所穿的衣服，不但華麗，而且清潔，一塵不染，不用洗濯。臨命終時，衣服邋遢，有了塵垢。

（三）腋下汗出：天人的身體，永不出汗。臨命終時，兩腋有汗水流出。

（四）身體臭穢：天人在往昔時，修行認眞，嚴持戒律，所以有一股戒香生出，常放芬香撲鼻的氣味。我們爲什麼有狐臭味？就因爲不守戒律。天人在臨命終時，則放出死屍的味道。

（五）不樂本座：天人時時在定中，如如不動，了了常明。當他看到自己四衰現象生出之後，知道死之將至，心亂如麻，妄想紛飛，坐立不安，站起坐

Five signs of decay appear when celestial beings are about to die:

1. Their flower garlands wilt. The elegant flower garlands worn by gods never wither. At the time of death, however, the flowers naturally wilt.

2. Their clothes become soiled. The clothes worn by the gods are gorgeous, clean, and dust-free; they don't need to be washed. But when the gods are about to die, their clothes become soiled and dirty.

3. Their armpits begin to perspire. Celestial beings' bodies never sweat. But at the time of their death, their armpits start to perspire.

4. Their bodies begin to stink. Since gods cultivated very diligently and upheld the precepts strictly, their bodies emit the "fragrance of the precepts"; they constantly give off a pleasant fragrance. Why do our bodies stink? Because we do not uphold the precepts. As their death approaches, however, celestial beings' bodies start to smell like corpses.

5. They cannot sit still. Celestial beings are perpetually in samadhi. Their bodies remain still and their minds are clear. But when they see the previous four signs of decay, they know their death is near. Thus their minds become confused and filled with random thoughts. They are fidgety— standing up and sitting down, sitting down and

下，坐下站起，往返幾次，就命終了，遂到六道輪迴受生。地獄業成熟了，就到地獄道去受生；餓鬼業成熟了，就到餓鬼道去受生；畜生業成熟了，就到畜生道去受生；阿修羅業成熟了，就到阿修羅道去受生；人業成熟了，就到人道去受生。可是每一道中，又有千差萬別的種類。以「人」來講，上自皇帝，下至乞丐，有種種不同的階級。有的富貴，有的貧賤，有的智慧，有的愚癡，有的長壽，有的夭亡，有的健康，有的多病，這都是業力所感。

standing up— and after doing that a few times, they die and fall into the six paths to be reborn. If the karma that destines them for the hells ripens, they will be reborn in the hells. If the karma that destines them to be hungry ghosts ripens, they will be reborn in the path of hungry ghosts. If their animal karma ripens, they will get reborn in the path of animals. If their *asura* karma ripens, they go to the path of the *asuras*. If their human karma ripens, they will become human beings. And within each path there are thousands upon thousand of variations. In the human path alone, there are different levels ranging from as high as an emperor to as low as a beggar. Some people are wealthy and noble, some are lowly and poor, some are wise, some are stupid, some enjoy long lives, some have short lives, some are healthy, and some are afflicted with illness. Those conditions are determined by the power of karma.

道場中要謹言慎行

不可有妒賢忌能的心，
不可障礙他人發菩提心。

無論哪一位，來到萬佛聖城，一定要謹言慎行，把
好名好利的心收拾起來。不要目空一切，認爲自己
了不起，把自己舉得高高在上，輕視其他人，這就
是貢高我慢的行爲。有這些邋遢東西，在心裏負擔
，在身上負擔，在精神上負擔，怎能成就道業？我
常對你們說：

　　　真認自己錯，莫論他人非；
　　　他非即我非，同體名大悲。

要看每個人和自己是一樣。人家的快樂，就是自己

152

Act and Speak with Prudence in a Way-place

We shouldn't envy talented people, nor should we obstruct people from bringing forth the Bodhi resolve.

Whoever you are, when you come to the City of Ten Thousand Buddhas, you must speak and act prudently. Subdue any thoughts of pursuing fame or benefit. Avoid arrogance. Don't regard yourself as somebody special, put yourself on a pedestal and look down on others. That is conceited behavior. How can you accomplish the Way if your mind, body, and spirit are influenced by such defiled attitudes? I constantly tell you,

> Truly recognize your own faults
> And don't discuss the faults of others.
> Others' faults are just my own;
> Being one with everyone is called
>   Great Compassion.

Regard everyone as being the same as yourself. Regard the

的快樂。人家的痛苦，就是自己的痛苦。人家做善事，等於我做善事一樣的高興；人家做惡事，等於我做惡事一樣的悲痛。要有這樣的思想，才能和人和平相處。規勸犯戒的人，勉勵守戒的人，不可有妒賢忌能的心，不可障礙他人發菩提心。

我出家之後，在道場工作，總是爭先恐後去做，絕對不到處宣揚，我做了什麼工？我做了什麼活？如果這樣表功，反而無功德。不像現在的人，做點工怕吃虧，做點事怕上當。自己覺得很聰明，其實是傻瓜。你一天所做的工，不用說，護法神記得清清楚楚。功德圓滿，自然有所感應，所謂：

有麝自然香，何須大風揚。

芸芸眾生，所犯的毛病，到做工的時候，就無我相；到吃飯的時候，就無人相；到打架的時候，就無眾生相；到吃肉的時候，就無壽者相。還大言不慚地說：「我吃你的肉，超度你上西天。」有這種思想的人，自己認爲是聰明，其實聰明反被聰明誤，

happiness of others as your own, and regard their sorrows as yours, too. "If people do good deeds, I'll rejoice as if I had done them; if people do evil deeds, I'll be as grieved as if I had done them." If we think that way, we'll get along harmoniously with others. In advising people who have broken precepts or encouraging people who uphold precepts, we shouldn't be jealous of those who are capable, nor should we obstruct others in bringing forth the Bodhi resolve.

After I became a monk, I strove to do whatever work needed to be done around the monastery. Had I advertised my merit, there would have been no merit. Nowadays people worry about taking a loss or being cheated when they do a little work. They consider themselves smart, but actually their attitude is foolish. There is no need to publicize the work you do each day; the Dharma-protecting spirits will know and remember it well. When your merit and virtue are complete, you will naturally have a response. It is said,

> Musk will naturally emit a fragrance;
> It doesn't need any wind to spread it.

Living beings have these faults: when they are supposed to work, they use the excuse of "no self"; during mealtimes, they act as if there are "no people" other than themselves; when it comes to fighting, they assume that there are "no living beings"; and when it comes to eating meat, they think that there is "no life." Yet, at the same time they shamelessly

上了大當，自己猶不知而已。

我們修行人，時時刻刻要攝心律己，舉動行爲管自己，行住坐臥不離家。不離家就是不找人家的毛病，不說人家的是非，也就是謹言慎行。時時迴光返照，刻刻反求諸己。去掉自己古怪脾氣，保留自己的忍辱功夫。千言萬語一句話，少說話多修行，不要自我宣傳，我怎樣！我怎樣！既然出了家，還有在家的習氣。那麼，出家爲了什麼？你們自己好好反省一下，應當不應當？

declare, "By eating your flesh I'll liberate you so you can go to the Western Pure Land." People think that is clever reasoning. Actually, though they don't realize it, they outsmart themselves and end up losing in a big way.

We cultivators should always focus our minds and discipline ourselves, watch our own conduct, and not "leave our home" in walking, standing, sitting or lying down. Not "leaving our home" means not looking at others' faults and not talking about others' rights and wrongs. It also means using caution in our words and conduct, always reflecting within and examining ourselves, getting rid of our idiosyncratic temperament, and developing the skill of patience. In short, talk less and cultivate more. Don't advertise yourself: "I'm like this! I'm like that!" If you continue to cling to your worldly habits after becoming a monk, then what's the point of becoming a monk? Think about it. Is that the way you ought to be?

修道人不可自私

現在大家要反省一下，
我在佛教中應該盡些什麼責任？

今天地藏七開始，每年農曆七月十五日（盂蘭盆法會）至七月三十日（地藏王菩薩聖誕），一連打兩個地藏七，超度孤魂野鬼往生，祈禱世界和平，這是我們萬佛聖城應盡的責任。

希望大家專心一致來念「南無地藏王菩薩」的聖號，念到心口相應的時候，一定能有所感應。不可一心二用，要集中精神來念。要是不至誠懇切地念，雖然不能說沒有功德，但是就少得多了。若能專一其心來念，便和地藏菩薩的聖號打成一片，念到「

Cultivators Must Be Unselfish

Now let us reflect for a moment:
What is my duty to Buddhism?

The Earth Store Recitation Session starts today. Every year from the fifteenth of the seventh month (Ullambana Dharma Assembly) to the thirtieth of that month (Birthday of Earth Store Bodhisattva) on the lunar calendar, we have two consecutive seven-day Earth Store Bodhisattva recitation sessions to rescue the lonely souls and wandering ghosts and to pray for world peace. That is a duty the City of Ten Thousand Buddhas should perform.

I hope everyone will recite the holy name "Namo Earth Store Bodhisattva" with concentration. When you recite to a state wherein mind and body correspond with each other, surely you will have a response. You cannot have your mind on two things. You must concentrate all your attention and energy to recite. If you do not recite with utmost sincerity,

不念而自念」的境界時，心中自然清淨而自在，什麼煩惱也沒有了。

修道人不能自私，不要有「懷其寶而迷其邦」的思想。得到好吃的食物，大家吃；得到好穿的衣服，大家穿；得到好住的房子，大家住；得到好的感應，要和大家分享，供養大家。凡是所有的功德，一定要迴向法界眾生，否則，就是自私。

如果有人得到好的感應，應該供養大家；得到不好的感應，也應該向大家說清楚，不要往自己臉上貼金，說我有什麼了不起的感應，更不可有微妙的感應就保留不說，有這兩種思想的人，都是「自私」在作祟。

現在大家要反省一下，我在佛教中應該盡些什麼責任？是不是在佛教中不管事，你推我，我推你，誰也不肯做？

我們人人要發心，以佛教為己任，佛教興衰，人人

then although I can't say you won't have any merit and virtue at all, there will be a lot less. If you can recite single-mindedly, you can become one with the holy name of Earth Store Bodhisattva. When you reach the state where the recitation continues automatically even when you aren't reciting, your mind will naturally be pure and at ease, and free of all afflictions.

Cultivators can't be selfish. Don't have an attitude of "reserving your talent and not using it to serve your country." When there's good food, it should be shared by everyone; when we get comfortable clothes, everyone should have the same to wear; when we get a nice place to live, everyone should live in it; when we attain positive responses, they should be shared with and offered to everyone. All merit and virtue should be transferred to the living beings of the Dharma Realm. Otherwise, it would be selfish.

If you attain positive responses, you should offer them to all. If you get undesirable responses, you should also make them clear to all. Don't brag about having extraordinary responses just to make yourself look good; on the other hand, if you do have a wonderful response don't keep it to yourself. People who act in those two ways are motivated by selfishness.

Now let us reflect for a moment: What is our duty to Buddhism? Should we ignore the work that is to be done, pushing it back and forth among ourselves so that no one ends up doing it?

Every one of us should resolve to consider Buddhism our

有責。不是說，那是他的事，不關我的事，與我沒
有關係。

爲佛教的利益，要犧牲一切，就是粉身碎骨，也在
所不辭。要有這種精神，才是眞正的佛教徒。不要
作「依佛吃飯、賴佛穿衣」的假佛教徒，要盡其所
能來擁護三寶，那就是沒有自私心。

不要有時時怕吃虧，刻刻怕上當的心理，總是把自
己看得很高，認爲了不起。要有爲法忘軀的精神，
才有資格作個佛教徒。

一九八三年八月二十五日
地藏七開示於萬佛聖城

own responsibility. The rise and fall of Buddhism is every-one's responsibility. You cannot say, "It's someone else's job, not mine. It has nothing to do with me!"

We should be willing to sacrifice everything, even our lives, for the sake of Buddhism. That is the spirit of a true Buddhist. Do not be a fake Buddhist--one who uses the Buddha's name only to get food and clothing. To be totally unselfish requires that you do everything you can to protect the Triple Jewel.

Avoid constantly worrying about suffering a loss or being cheated. Don't think highly of yourself and consider yourself so special. Be prepared to forget yourself for the sake of the Dharma; then you deserve to be called a Buddhist.

A talk given on August 25, 1983,
during an Earth Store Recitation Session
at the City of Ten Thousand Buddhas

效法地藏王菩薩

都是往真處來做，
絕對沒有絲毫虛僞。

地藏王菩薩的願力最大，他說：

> 地獄未空，誓不成佛；
> 眾生度盡，方證菩提。

這種精神多麼慈悲。菩薩對我們眾生非常關心，無
微不至。凡是對佛教有信心的人，努力修行的人，
地藏王菩薩會在該行者的禪定之中，或夢寐之中，
現身爲他說法。可惜我們不了解菩薩的用心，反而
辜負菩薩的慈悲，實在對不起菩薩。可是菩薩不生
氣，原諒愚癡眾生，仍然不休息普度眾生，將眾生

Follow the Example of Earth Store Bodhisattva

Everything a Bodhisattva does is sincere, devoid of the slightest trace of hypocrisy.

Earth Store Bodhisattva has the greatest vows. He has said,

> As long as the hells are not empty,
>   I will not become a Buddha.
> Only when all living beings have been completely
>   liberated will I become a Buddha.

What a compassionate spirit! This Bodhisattva cares tremendously about us living beings. If someone has faith in Buddhism and applies effort in cultivation, the Bodhisattva will appear in that cultivator's samadhi or dreams and speak Dharma for him. However, we fail to understand the Bodhisattva's intentions and appreciate his compassion. We sorely disappoint him, but he doesn't get angry. He forgives foolish living beings and continues liberating them

度盡，他才成佛。

菩薩所做的事情，都是往真處來做，絕對沒有絲毫虛偽，純粹為救眾生離苦得樂。

現在打地藏七，誰有真心，誰就有感應；誰有誠意，誰就有受用。這個受用，並不是得到神通妙用，而是心中清淨，沒有妄想。沒有妄想，便有感應道交的境界現前。有人說：「平安就是感應；知錯就是感應；比以前更聰明，這是感應；比以前更能幹，這是感應。」說得不錯，就是這樣的情形。

all without rest. Only after all living beings are liberated will he become a Buddha.

A Bodhisattva does everything with the sincere intent to save beings, alleviate their suffering, and bring them happiness. He is devoid of the slightest trace of hypocrisy.

Now we are having an Earth Store Bodhisattva session, and whoever is true-hearted will have a response. Whoever is sincere will benefit. Benefit doesn't mean attaining spiritual penetrations, but having a pure, clear mind with no false thoughts. If there are no false thoughts, states of responsive interaction with the Way will appear. Some say, "Peace is a response; recognizing one's faults is a response; becoming smarter than before is a response; becoming more capable than before is response." Well said! That's just how it is.

忍受無理的攻擊

在逆境中撐扎，
仍不灰心，照常精進。

我現在對大家說一說我念《地藏經》的經過。我在
十六歲那年，開始爲人講《六祖壇經》和《金剛經
》。我根本不會講，可是還要講，爲什麼？因爲當
時有很多人想研究經典，可是不識字。於是我想，
我應該擔任這份工作，所以義不容辭講起難講的經
典。

有一天，在偶然機會之下，發現一本《地藏菩薩本
願經》，如獲至寶。念了一遍，覺得地藏菩薩太慈
悲！菩薩對我們這樣地關心，可是我們還不知道。
於是我發心，天天念一部《地藏經》，又發心跪在

Endure Unjustified Attacks

Don't be disheartened by bad states.
Don't give up; always keep advancing.

Let me tell you my story about reciting the *Sutra of the Past Vows of Earth Store Bodhisattva*. When I was seventeen years old, I started lecturing on the *Sixth Patriarch's Platform Sutra* and the *Vajra Sutra*. I didn't know how to lecture, but I still went ahead. Why? Because at that time, there were a lot of people who wanted to study Sutras, but couldn't read. So I thought I should take up this job. I acted from a strong sense of duty and started explaining these difficult Sutras.

One day I chanced to come upon the *Sutra of the Past Vows of Earth Store Bodhisattva*. I felt like I had acquired a most precious gem. I read the Sutra once and felt that Earth Store Bodhisattva was truly compassionate. He cares about us so much, yet we don't even realize it. So I made a vow to recite the Sutra once every day, kneeling down in front of the

佛前念。佛殿是用磚塊鋪地，沒有墊子，我只穿一層布的褲子，跪在磚地上，念一部經約需兩小時。只顧念經，膝蓋跪破了，也不知道痛，愈念愈高興。每天準時跪在佛前，虔誠地念。一百多天之後，終因發生魔障而停止。

修道人，如果不用功修行，就沒有魔來考驗，稍有點成就，魔就來考驗你是否有定力？

當我在念《地藏經》時，有位居士來到廟上供養，見我跪著念經，很讚歎我，很羨慕我，所以對廟上的人說：「他這麼用功，這麼精進……。」

等這位居士走了之後，廟裏的和尚都來罵我：「你裝模作樣！故意給居士們看，表示自己是老修行，這是攀緣！」當時我不辯論，自己心裏明白，乃是為修行而念經。可是從此之後，無理取鬧的事情，常常發生。在念經之前，他們來罵我：「假裝修行。」念完之後，他們又罵我：「裝修行裝完啦！」冷嘲熱諷，天天如此。但我忍可於心，一言不發。

Buddha. The Buddha Hall had a brick floor and there were no cushions. The pants I wore had only one layer of cloth, and I knelt on the brick floor in them. It took about two hours to recite the Sutra once. I concentrated only on reciting and didn't notice that my knees were scraped and sore from kneeling. I didn't even feel pain, I was just happy reciting. The more I recited the happier I became. Every day I would punctually kneel in front of the Buddha to sincerely recite the Sutra. Over a hundred days later, a demonic obstruction occurred, so I stopped reciting.

If cultivators don't work hard at cultivation, no demons will come to test them. But if you have some accomplishment, demons will come and test you to see if you have any samadhi power. When I was reciting the *Earth Store Sutra*, a layperson came to the monastery to make offerings. Seeing me reciting the Sutra kneeling down, he praised me, expressed his admiration of me in public and said to people at the temple, "He works so hard, so vigorously..." After the layperson left, all the monks of the monastery came over to scold me. "You pretender! You did that deliberately to make the laypeople think that you're a seasoned cultivator. That is exploiting conditions!" I didn't argue. In my mind I knew that I recited for the sake of cultivation. But from then on I was hassled constantly. When I started reciting the Sutra, they'd come by and scold me, "Pretending!" After I was done, they scolded me again, "So, you finished pretending!" Every day they took turns in taunting and jeering at me. But I just endured it and didn't say anything.

念到一百多天之後，真的魔障來了。某日剛剛念完一部《地藏經》，大師兄來到我的面前，打了我一頓，我莫名其妙，也不敢發問，然後，他罵：「你這個東西，在這裏躲懶偷安，人家在工作，你裝模作樣在念經，表演給人看。廟上哪有你修行的地方？你有什麼功德在這裏修行？」所以，我只好停止念《地藏經》。

今天又逢打地藏七的日子，使我想起往事。修道不容易，時時都會遇到障礙。你們大家很幸運，能遇到這樣理想的修道處所，不受人罵，不受人打，多麼自在，更要學你們師父那樣在逆境中掙扎，仍不灰心，照常精進。

After I had recited for over a hundred days, a real demonic obstacle came along. One day when I had just finished reciting the Sutra, a senior Dharma brother came over and whacked me. I was confused but dared not ask what was going on. He scolded, "You! Hiding here and being lazy. Other people are working and you're here showing off, pretending to be reciting a Sutra. Is this temple a place for you to cultivate? What merit and virtue do you have to be cultivating here?" So I stopped my recitation of the *Earth Store Sutra*.

Now that we are again having an Earth Store Bodhisattva recitation session, I am reminded of the past. It's not easy to cultivate. You encounter obstacles all the time. You are very lucky that you can come to this ideal Way-place where you aren't scolded or beaten. How comfortable! You should learn to be like your teacher; don't be disheartened by bad states. Don't give up; always keep advancing.

感化婦人孝公婆

因你不孝順公婆的緣故，
所以你的小孩子病了。

我在東北三緣寺依止常仁大師（王孝子）的時候，
有一次因為建廟，便到村莊借車運建築材料。離廟
十五里有個村莊，叫大灞。當時正是春耕的時候，
農人很忙，所以沒有借到車。我到村長家裏，他也
說現在太忙了，哪有時間為廟上去運料？

就在這時，村長的弟媳來見我。她說：「老修行，
我的小孩子病了，醫生不能治。您能不能發慈悲心
，把我小孩子的病治好？」

我對她說：「因你不孝順公婆（丈夫的父母）的緣

174

How One Woman Became a Filial Daughter-in-law

Because she had been unfilial to her parents-in-law, her child became ill.

When I was in Manchuria, I went to stay with Great Master Chang Ren (Filial Son Wang) at Three Conditions Monastery. Once when the temple was under construction, I went to a nearby village to borrow some carts for transporting construction materials. About five miles from the temple, there was a village called Daba. It was spring, tilling time. The farmers were very busy, and I couldn't come up with any carts. I went to the village leader's house. He said, "We're really busy now. How can we find time to transport materials for a temple?"

Then his sister-in-law came to see me. She said, "Old cultivator, my child is sick and the doctors can do nothing. Can you be merciful and cure my child's illness?"

I told her, "Your child is ill because you've been unfilial to

175

故，所以你的小孩子病了。你想要小孩子病好，一定要懺悔——在祖先牌位前叩頭祈禱：『自今以後，孝敬公婆，和睦妯娌。』然後跪在公婆面前認錯：『發誓不惹公婆生煩惱。』如果真心去做，妳的小孩子一定會好。」

她即時照樣做了，可是小孩子病還沒有好轉。她又跑來見我，敘述這種情形，我對她說：「妳把小孩子抱來給我看看！」她立刻把小孩子抱來，是一個年約三、四歲的小男孩，眼睛閉著，嘴巴張著。我在小孩的頭頂拍三下，不一會兒工夫，小孩子睜開眼睛，東看西望。約過了五分鐘，便離開他媽媽的懷抱，下地能跑跳，活潑如初。

這時村長高興地對我說：「老修行！您把我姪兒的病治好，我們全村的車，明天到廟上幫忙運材料。」第二天早晨，來了九輛大車，晚上回去的時候，有輛車的騾子被壓到而腿跛。車主感到奇怪，他在想：「替廟上做工，應當有功德，為什麼反遭意外之災？」他百思不解這個因果，乃來問我：「老修

your parents-in-law. If you want him to get well, you must repent. Kneel and bow in front of the ancestral tablets and pray. From now on, be filial and respectful to your parents-in-law, and be amicable with your sisters-in-law. Kneel before your parents-in-law and confess your faults, and vow not to distress them again. If you do that with a sincere heart, your child will get well."

She immediately did as she was told. But the child did not get better, so she came to see me again and described the situation. I told her, "Bring your child here and let me take a look at him." She brought her child over at once. The child was a boy of about three or four years of age. His eyes were shut, but his mouth was open. I tapped the little boy three times on the head. After a while he opened his eyes and looked around. About five minutes later, he jumped down from his mother's arms and ran around as if he had never been sick.

The village leader then said to me happily, "Old cultivator, you cured my nephew's sickness. Tomorrow, all carts from the village will go to the temple to help you transport materials." The next morning, nine large carts showed up. But that evening, as the carts were being returned, a mule pulling one of the carts hurt its leg, which caused it to limp. The owner couldn't understand it. He thought, "Working for the temple should have created a lot of merit and virtue. How come this accident occurred instead?" He couldn't

行，這是什麼緣故？」

我對車主說：「你不要著急，你的騾腿雖然撞傷，不久就會好的，這可是救了你家人的性命。」他聽了我這樣說，很受感動，決定第二天再來運材料。

這件事發生之後，無論到哪個村莊借車運材料，他們都樂意幫忙，知道給廟上做工能有無量的功德，甚至有的人，爭先恐後出車出人來到廟上作功德。

一九八三年八月二十六日

understand the cause and effect, so he came and asked, "Old cultivator, what's the reason for this?"

I told him, "Don't worry. Even though your mule hurt its leg, it will get well soon. But the life of your family was saved." When he heard that, he was moved and decided to come and help again the next day.

After that incident, no matter what village I approached to borrow carts for transporting materials, the people there were all willing to help. Knowing that there was boundless merit and virtue in working for the temple, people were eager to lend their carts and men.

A talk given on August 26, 1983

放下屠刀成孝子

我們兩人相見，對坐一小時，
一句話沒有說。

我在東北家鄉，曾遇見一位孝子，他姓尤，名智惠。以前是大盜，打家劫舍，綁票勒索，無惡不作。有一天，他身受重傷，從死裏逃生，遂良心發現，生大慚愧，於是決定革面洗心，重新做人，發願說：「如果不死，一定到父母墳前守孝。」不久傷癒，便回到家中，在父母墓旁，建一間茅棚，在那裏住了幾年。

有一年夏天，天降大雨，氾濫成災。他發心禱告上天，如果三天內雨停天晴，我願割肉祭天。他又一想，等天晴再祭天，那是賄賂的行為，應該現在就

Putting Down the Cleaver and Becoming a Filial Son

One year we met. We sat face to face for an hour without speaking a word.

In my home town in Manchuria, I met a filial son by the name of You Zhihui. He had been an outlaw involved in plundering, looting, kidnapping, extortion, and every sort of evil. One day he was badly injured. He was on the verge of death, but he then recovered. Thereupon he discovered his conscience and became greatly ashamed. He decided to change himself and reform, to become a totally new person. He also vowed, "If I don't die, I'm determined to practice filial piety by staying by my parents' grave in mourning." Not long afterwards, his wound healed. He returned home, built a hut by his parents' grave, and lived there for some years.

One summer, the area was flooded by torrential rain. He resolved his mind and prayed to heaven, "If it stops raining within three days, I will cut my flesh as a sacrifice to

割肉祭天，來表示至誠之心。於是擺上香案，祈禱上天，保佑這地方的老百姓，令他們秋天豐收。遂舉刀將乳下之肉割下，因流血過多，昏倒於地，人事不知。

彼愚誠之心，感動天地，奇蹟出現，立刻雨過天青！家人來送飯，發現他臥在血地上。把他喚醒，替他療傷。約有半個月，傷口痊癒。

在這半個月之間，有隻可愛的小鳥，天天飛到他的床前，來安慰他，唱歌：「多作德！多作德！作德多好！」與他成為好朋友。半個月以後，小鳥不知飛向何處去了。愚誠所至，霪雨即停，神鳥為伴，這種境界不可思議。

有一年，我們兩人相見，對坐一小時，一句話沒有說。為什麼？因為沒有什麼可說的，一切盡在不言中。他知道我，我知道他，心照不宣，只可意會，不可言傳。

我到臺灣去弘法，遇到水果和尚（廣欽老法師）也

heaven." Then he thought that waiting until it stopped raining to worship heaven would be a case of bribing; to show his utmost sincerity he should do it straightaway. So he prepared an incense altar and prayed for heaven to protect the people of that area and let them have a good harvest. Then he took a knife and cut some of his flesh from his chest. Due to profuse bleeding, he passed out on the ground.

His sincerity moved heaven and earth. A miracle happened: the rain stopped right away. When his family brought food over and found him lying unconscious in a pool of blood, they woke him up and tended to his wound. Half a month later the wound healed. During that half month, a delightful little bird flew to his bedside every day to comfort him, singing, "Do more merit! Do more merit! How wonderful it is to do merit!" and became a good friend to him. Half a month later, the bird was gone. His utmost sincerity stopped the pouring rain and brought the company of a divine bird. It was an inconceivable state.

One year we met. We sat face to face for an hour without speaking a word. Why? Because there was nothing to be said. Everything was in the unspoken. He understood me and I understood him. We had a tacit agreement. It could only be comprehended, not expressed by words.

When I went to Taiwan to propagate the Buddhadharma and met the Fruit Monk (Elder Dharma Master Guangqin),

是這樣的情形，相對無語，可是心中有無限的欣悅，這是心靈感應作用。所謂「心心相印」，彼此通達，無所障礙。

the same thing happened. We sat face to face without speaking, but there was boundless joy in our hearts; such was the wonderful functioning of responding minds. It was what's known as "the mind certifying the mind" in unhindered communication.

人生必經的過程

「生從何處來，死往何處去」的問題，
把它研究明白，就能出離三界，
不受輪迴。

每個人一生要經過「生老病死」四大苦，任何人也
逃不出這四種苦。除非你修道，了生脫死，那又另
當別論，可是一般人都要受這四苦。

「生」的時候，好像兩山相夾，所以小孩出生時，
首先要哭，表示苦的意思。生時，親友被生的境界
所轉，大家來慶祝，雖然賀喜，其實是苦。

「老」的時候，眼睛花了，耳朵也聾了，牙齒也掉
了，頭髮也白了。手腳不聽指揮，互相罷工，不能
動彈，這也是很痛苦。

186

The Inevitable Course of Life

Where do we come from at birth, and where we go to at death? We investigate this question until we understand; then we can leave the Three Realms and avoid further transmigration.

In the course of one's life, everyone must go through the four great sufferings of birth, old age, sickness and death. No one can escape these four kinds of suffering, unless they cultivate the Way and end birth and death-then it's another story. But ordinary people all have to undergo these four sufferings.

Birth is like being sandwiched between two mountains. That's why the first thing babies do when they are delivered is cry. Crying indicates suffering. When there is a birth, relatives and friends are moved by the event and all come to celebrate. Although people think of birth as a cause for celebration, it's actually suffering.

In old age, the eyes become blurred, the ears grow deaf, teeth fall out, hair turns gray. The limbs are out of control; they go on strike and can't move. That state is very painful.

「病」的時快，四大失調，互不合作，乃至臥床不能起。如果貧病交加，更是苦上加苦。那時候，心有餘而力不足，你說苦不苦？

到「死」的時候，其苦更無法表達，簡直如活牛剝皮，爲兒女牽腸掛肚，被七情六欲所迷，還是放不下。其實「死」是人生必經的途徑，何必生時歡喜死時愁呢？可惜一般愚癡的人，打不破這種執著。

我們現在要研究「生從何處來，死往何處去」的問題。把它研究明白，就能出離三界，不受輪迴。

釋迦牟尼佛就爲研究這個問題而出家修道。訪道六年，苦修六年，沒有得到解決生死的方法。最後在菩提樹下靜坐四十九天，夜睹明星而悟道，徹底明白生命之輪——「十二因緣」。

今天爲什麼說這些道理？因爲我初到香港（一九四九年）時，最先皈依的弟子就是羅果明居士。她今年八十一歲，昨天早晨往生，使我有所感觸。她一

During sickness, the four elements are imbalanced and un-cooperative, sometimes to the point of causing one to be bedridden. If poverty is added to sickness, the suffering is aggravated. At that time, the spirit is willing but the flesh is weak. What do you say: Is that not suffering?

The agony of death is beyond words. It is as great as that of a cow being flayed alive. Deluded by the seven emotions and the six desires, you worry about the children and cannot let go of your attachments. Death is something we must go through. What need is there to rejoice at the time of birth and mourn at the time of death? Unfortunately, most people are too foolish to break through those attachments.

Where do we come from at birth, and where do we go to at death? We must investigate that question until we understand; then we can leave the Three Realms and avoid further transmigration.

Shakyamuni Buddha renounced his home in order to pursue that question. For six years he sought the Way and under-took ascetic practices, yet he still found no solution to the problem of birth and death. Finally, he sat in meditation beneath the Bodhi tree for forty-nine days, saw a bright star one night and got enlightened. He thoroughly understood the wheel of life–the Twelve Causal Conditions.

Why do I tell you this today? When I first arrived in Hong Kong in 1949, the first person who took refuge with me was

生受環境壓迫，但是從不向環境投降，自己忍苦耐勞養育五個兒女，兒女都有相當的成就，羅果明居士也得以含笑於九泉之下，或者往生於極樂世界。

一九八三年九月四日

Upasika Luo Guoming. This year she turned eighty-one years old. She passed away yesterday morning, and that brought some thoughts to my mind. All her life she was oppressed by circumstances, but she never gave up. She bore suffering and hardship patiently, and brought up five children. Her sons and daughters all have considerable achievement. Therefore, she ought to be able to rest in peace, or be reborn in the Land of Ultimate Bliss.

A talk given on September 4, 1983

一本難念的經

若貪戀紅塵，以為樂事，
那麼這本難念的經，就永遠也念不完。

所謂「家家都有一本難念的經」，這本經什麼時候能念完？什麼時候能不難念？誰也不知道。

我們修道的人，可以說把這本難念的經，已經念完了。現在念的經，是容易念的經。

我今天對大家說這個因緣，提醒大家要認識「生老病死」的問題。遇到這種境界，要想得開，放得下，不要被境界所纏縛。最好對境無心，視為平常。人能不動心，就是如如不動，了了常明。

A Difficult Sutra to Read

If we crave worldly pleasures,
we'll never finish reading this difficult Sutra.

It is said, "Every family has a Sutra that's hard to read." [Every family has a skeleton in the closet.] When can we finish reading this Sutra? Or when will this Sutra not be so hard to read? No one knows. We cultivators can say that we have finished reading this difficult Sutra. Now we are reading the easy Sutras.

Today I tell you of these causes and conditions, reminding you to recognize the question of birth, old age, sickness, and death. When we encounter these states, we should be able to put them down and not be bound by them. It is best if you can face a state with no mind, regarding it as something ordinary. If you can remain unmoved in your mind, then you are in a state of unmoving thusness and clear and constant understanding.

世間的人，都被境界所轉，而不能轉境界。所以漫無目標，拿不定宗旨，糊糊塗塗一輩子，生來糊塗，死去糊塗。所以上一回當，不知覺悟，又上一回當，在六道中流轉，好像賭錢一樣，賭輸了還想下注。

所謂「省吃儉用下大注。」凡夫總想孤注一擲，將所輸的錢，一下子贏回來，可是越賭越輸，越輸越賭，乃至陷在淤泥中，拔不出腿來。結果傾家蕩產，把本有的家珍、自性的法寶，統統丟掉了，還不知返本還原，也不知迴光返照，反迷歸覺；更不知背塵合覺。在人世間，生了又死，死了又生，在生死苦海中掙扎。努力向上爬，剛剛爬出頭，又掉下去。如此周而復始，永無了期。

出家人就要努力修行，否則，逃不出六道輪迴。若能急流勇退，知道賭錢不是好事，所謂「浪子回頭金不換」，這時，曉得「誰賭博誰輸錢，不賭博就贏錢」的真理。好像下棋，總有輸贏，下棋的人，

People in this world are often influenced by situations, instead of being the ones who influence situations. That's why they are aimless and cannot hold on to their principles. People are born muddled, live their whole lives muddled, and die muddled. We are cheated once, don't learn anything from it, and come back to be cheated again; in that way we revolve in the six paths. It's like gambling-you've already lost but you still want to make bets.

There's a saying, "Live frugally so you can place a big bet." Trying to win back their lost money, ordinary people always want to stake everything on one bet. But the more you gamble the more you lose, and the more you lose the more you want to gamble, until you find yourself sinking in quicksand, unable to pull yourself out. In the end you lose everything, including your family heirlooms and the Dharma treasures of your own nature. All is lost, and still you fail to return to the source and go back to the origin. You don't reflect within and return from delusion to enlightenment; you don't unite with enlightenment and go against the dust. Being born and dying in this world again and again, you struggle in the bitter sea of birth and death. You strive to climb out, but just as you get your head above the waves, you're submerged again. Thus the cycle goes on, never coming to an end.

Those of you who have entered the monastic life must cultivate diligently, otherwise you won't be able to escape rebirth in the six paths. If you can quickly withdraw, and

195

永遠不是輸，永遠不是贏。這種哲理，令我們對境明心，因事悟道。

各位善知識！要痛念生死，發菩提心，不要再在苦海中浮沉。凡是不願離開苦海的人，便是愚癡人。若貪戀紅塵，以爲樂事，那麼這本難念的經，就永遠也念不完。我們已經出了家，不要再念這本念不完的經。

know that gambling is no good, then as the saying goes, "The return of a prodigal son is something that even gold can't buy." At that time you will know the truth of the saying, "Whoever gambles, loses money; whoever doesn't gamble, wins money." Just as in chess, there are always winners and losers. A chess player won't always lose, nor will he always win. With that principle, we can understand our mind and awaken to the Way as we face situations.

Good advisors: Take birth and death seriously, develop the Bodhi mind, and stop bobbing up and down in the sea of suffering. People who aren't willing to leave the sea of suffering are fools. If we crave worldly pleasures, we'll never finish reading this difficult Sutra. We have already left the home life, so we shouldn't waste time reading this difficult Sutra that can never be finished.

培養高尚的人格

青年人要有一股英雄的氣概，
浩氣沖天的威儀。

各位小朋友！你們應該效法聖人，效法賢人，效法頂天立地大丈夫，效法古今中外大英雄。應效法他們的人格、道德，效法他們的學問、佛業。

你們現在是學習時期，在課堂學習知識和技能，在課外訓練道德和人格。豐富知識健全人格，將來可做一番轟轟烈烈的大事業，為全世界人類謀幸福。所謂「練達人情皆學問」，處處都要有經驗，能有進步，不要怕失敗，失敗是成功之母。

198

Develop a Noble Character

Young people should have a heroic spirit and a gallant and noble bearing.

Young friends! You should take the sages, worthy ones, great men of indomitable spirit, and ancient and contemporary heroes of all countries as your role models. Emulate them in their character, their virtue, their knowledge, and their Buddhist deeds.

You are now in the stage of learning: You acquire knowledge and skills in the classroom, and beyond the classroom you develop your virtue and character. Broaden your knowledge and strengthen your integrity, and in the future you'll accomplish great things and contribute to the happiness and welfare of all humankind. As it's said, "Tactfulness in human relationships is also a form of knowledge." You must gain experience in all aspects of life. Forge ahead without fear of failure, for failure is the mother of success.

青年人要有一股英雄的氣概，浩氣沖天的威儀，將來必定能成爲演說家，傑出的弘法人才。

你們現在正是打基礎的時期，不但要把學問的基礎打好，也要把人格的基礎打好，人格的基礎比學問的基礎更爲重要。古人說：「聖人不死，大亂不止。」人有學問沒有人格，可以造反，爲害國家，使全天下大亂，所以要培養高尚的人格，將來爲人類服務，定能利益眾生。

欲奠定人格的基礎，先要說正直的話，不要說假話。切記！不說討人歡喜的話，不說違背良心的話。該說話時，一定要說；不應該說話時，一定不要說。要知道「言多必失」的道理。所謂「病從口入，禍從口出。」謹之！慎之！

孟子給我們立下人格三大標準。他說：

> 富貴不能婬，
> 貧賤不能移，
> 威武不能屈。

Young people should have a heroic spirit and a gallant and noble bearing. That way you will certainly become great speakers and outstanding propagators of the Dharma.

Now is the time for you to build your foundation. You should build a good foundation not only of knowledge, but also of character. The foundation of your character is more important than the foundation of knowledge. The ancients said, "Sages never die, and chaos never ceases." People who have knowledge but lack good character will be rebellious, and that will harm the country and cause chaos throughout the world. We must develop a noble character, so that in the future we can serve humanity and definitely benefit living beings.

To establish the foundation of character we should first of all speak truthfully, never falsely. Remember this! Don't say things just to please people, and don't say anything that goes against your conscience. When it's time for you to talk, then talk; when it's time for you to remain silent, don't talk. You should know that "he who talks a lot, errs a lot." It's also said, "Diseases enter through the mouth; misfortunes issue from it." So be careful!

Mencius set three great standards for character. He said,

> When wealthy, I will not indulge;
> When poor, I will not compromise my principles;
> When intimidated, I will not submit.

在富貴的時候，要守規矩，也就是不婬亂。在貧賤的時候，不改變志氣，也就是不被境界所轉。在威武勢力壓迫之下，不屈服不投降，也就是名利來誘惑也不變節。要有這種至大至剛做人的志氣，才能成為一個有用的人。

一九八三年九月四日
對學生開示於萬佛聖城

When you are wealthy, be self-disciplined and refrain from licentiousness. When in poverty, don't alter your resolve; that is, don't be influenced by circumstances. When oppressed by those with power, don't cower or surrender. Faced with the lure of fame or benefit, don't compromise your integrity. With such adamantine determination to be an ethical person, you will be able to make useful contributions to the world.

A talk given on September 4, 1983,
to students at the City of Ten Thousand Buddhas

萬丈高樓從地起

國家的能源不足，
基礎不堅，焉能強國？

小朋友！你們要知道萬丈高樓，是從平地一點一點
建築起來的；百丈的大樹，是一寸一寸長高的；人
，也是一天一天長成的。在小的時候，先要立志願
，本著目標，向前邁進。如果沒有目標、沒有宗旨
，好像「盲人騎瞎馬，夜半臨深淵。」你說危險不
危險？

兒童好像潔白的布，「染於蒼則蒼，染於黃則黃。
」隨著教育環境而轉變。所謂「近朱者赤，近墨者
黑。」受環境的薰染而改變。在《三字經》上說：

Skyscrapers Are Built from the Ground Up

If a nation's resources are inadequate and its foundation is shaky, how can the nation be strong?

Young friends! You know that skyscrapers are built little by little from the ground up. Hundred-foot-tall trees grew inch by inch before reaching such a height. People also grow day by day. In our youth, we should set our goals and then advance to fulfill them. Without goals or principles, we are like a blind man riding a blind horse coming upon an abyss at midnight. Wouldn't you say that is dangerous?

Children are like a piece of pure white cloth that becomes blue if dyed blue and yellow if dyed yellow. Children are transformed according to their educational environment. As it's said, "If you get near rouge, you'll turn red. If you touch ink, you'll turn black." Likewise children are influenced by their surroundings. The *Three Character Classic* says: "People at birth are by nature good. Their natures are

「人之初，性本善。性相近，習相遠。苟不教，性乃遷。」就是這個道理。

你們在萬佛聖城受教育，能不爭、不貪、不求、不自私、不自利、不妄語，將來對於社會、國家，一定有所貢獻。我們萬佛聖城成立的法界佛教大學、培德中學、育良小學都以此六大宗旨作為校訓。

大、中、小學各位老師！你們要念茲在茲教育第二代，這是神聖的工作，要教育學生做到盡善盡美的人格，實實在在的學問，將來就不會作嬉皮、流氓，不會作無賴、強盜，而作規規矩矩的好公民。現在教育失敗，為什麼？因為功利主義在作怪，一般人辦學校以賺錢為目的，以為學生越多越好，卻喪失教育崇高的宗旨。

各位老師！要用「幼吾幼以及人之幼」的精神來教育學生。兒童是國家的能源，國家的基礎；國家的能源不足基礎不堅，焉能強國？願共勉之！

similar, but their habits set them apart. If not taught properly, their natures will change." That's the principle here.

You are now being educated at the City of Ten Thousand Buddhas. If you can learn not to fight, not to be greedy, not to seek, not to be selfish, not to pursue personal advantage, and not to lie, in the future you will surely make a contribution to your society and country. These Six Guidelines are the motto for the schools at the City of Ten Thousand Buddhas: Dharma Realm Buddhist University, Developing Virtue Secondary School, and Instilling Goodness Elementary School.

Teachers at the university and the secondary and elementary schools! Sincerely devote yourself to educating the next generation. It's a sacred calling. If you can educate students so that they have perfect characters and solid knowledge, they won't turn into hippies, vagrants, bums, or robbers, but into good citizens. At present, the educational system has failed. Why? Because a utilitarian outlook has taken over. People open schools for the purpose of making money, so their attitude is: The more students the better. But what happens is that the noble purpose of education is lost.

All of you teachers should teach the students as if they were your own children. Children are the resources of the nation, the foundation of the country. If a nation's resources are inadequate and its foundation is weak, how can the nation become a strong one? Let's urge one another on!

好好讀書就是盡孝道

一切要腳踏實地的學習，
就是一分鐘的光陰，也不可空過。

這次觀音七，有很多學生參加，你們要明白孝順父母的道理。在家時，要聽從父母的話，幫助母親整理房間，收拾乾淨，幫助父親剪草等，做些應該做的事。在學校時，要聽老師的教誨，專心聽講，用功學習，不要把大好光陰錯過。一天認識一個字，一天學會一句文法，這就是孝順父母的表現。

你們要記住！在學校做個好學生，回到家中，做個好兒女。不但要聽父母的教誨，而且又要聽年長的人教導。要孝順父母，要恭敬年長的人，因為他的

208

To Study Hard Is to Be Filial

Diligently apply yourself to your studies and don't waste even a single minute.

There are many students attending this Guanyin recitation session, and you students should understand the principle of being filial to parents. At home, listen to your parents, help your mother clean the rooms and tidy the house, help your father mow the lawn, and do the chores that you are supposed to do. At school, listen to the teacher's instructions, concentrate during classes, study hard, and don't waste precious time. To learn a new word or a new grammar rule every day is also a way of being filial to your parents.

Remember to be a good student in school and a good child at home. You should listen not only to your parents' instructions, but also to the guidance of your elders. Be filial to your parents and respectful toward your elders, since

經驗比你們多，他的學問比你豐富。你們必須向他學習，作爲榜樣，才會有光明的前途。否則，前途就黯淡無光，沒有希望。

學生們要抱定目標，立定志願，要有堅忍不拔、百折不回的精神，將來才能轟轟烈烈的做一番大事業。成爲出乎其類，拔乎其萃的大豪傑。念書的時候，要用功讀書，不可貪玩、不可調皮、不要虛度光陰，要認眞學習一切技能。這樣才對得起父母，對得起師長，對得起學校。

你們要知道，這是佛教學校，專門教育良才，將來成爲世界上最有用的人。希望你們爲世界人類謀幸福，不可把世界給弄壞了。這是本校的希望。你們在這裏讀書，一切要腳踏實地的學習，就是一分鐘的光陰，也不可空過，所謂：

> 書山有路勤爲徑；
> 學海無涯苦作舟。

以此作你們的座右銘。

they have more experience and knowledge than you do. You should learn from them and take them as your models so that you can have a promising future. Otherwise your future will be dim and hopeless.

You students should set your goals, resolve your mind, and approach your studies with a persevering and unfaltering attitude so that in the future you'll be able to achieve great things and become outstanding heroes. When it's time for you to study, you should study diligently. Don't goof off, get into mischief, or waste time; instead, be earnest in learning all skills. That way you won't disappoint your parents, your teachers, or the school.

You should understand that this is a Buddhist school. It specializes in educating students to become good and productive citizens in the world. I hope that in the future you'll try to work for the welfare of all of the people in the world, not mess things up in the world. That's our hope at this school. As a student here, you must diligently apply yourself to your studies and not waste even a single minute. Your motto should be:

> With diligence, one forges a path
> through the mountain of books;
> By studying hard, one can cross
> the boundless ocean of knowledge.

211

你們要有堅苦耐勞的心，不可躲懶偷安，要養成勤儉的習慣，對於一張紙、一支筆，也要愛惜，不可隨便糟蹋。生活上要有規律，早睡早起，少看電視，多看益智良書。在學校學的功課，回到家中，一定要把它做完，時時溫習，所謂「溫故而知新」。看一遍有一遍的好處，不可看無益的連環圖畫小人書。

在中國東漢時，有個小孩子，名叫孔融，非常聰明，又知道孝道。有一天，朋友送來一筐梨。他的哥哥們選擇大梨吃。他才四歲，就知道「禮讓」的道理，於是他選擇一個小梨吃。他父親問他：「爲什麼不拿大梨呢？」孔融說：「因爲我年紀小，可以吃小梨，把大梨留著父母長輩吃。」你們想一想，孔融才四歲，就知道謙讓、友愛、孝順。有這種的德行，非一般的小孩可比的。這種美名，流傳千古，人人皆曉，所謂「融四歲，能讓梨」。

在東漢時，又有一個兒童，名叫黃香，他九歲的時候，母親死了，他對父親非常孝順。在冬天的時候

Be patient and persevering, never lazy. Learn to be frugal. Cherish even a sheet of paper or a pen. You should lead disciplined lives: Go to bed early and rise early, watch less television, read plenty of good books, finish your homework after you come home, and constantly review what you have learned. It is said, "Reviewing what you have learned will aid you in learning new knowledge." You derive benefit every time you review. Don't read useless comic books.

During the Eastern Han dynasty [A.D. 25 - 219] in China, there was a child named Kong Rong. He was very bright and understood the principle of filiality. One day a friend brought over a basket of pears. His elder brothers picked the large ones to eat. Rong was four years old, yet he already knew the principle of yielding to others. So he took a small pear. His father asked him, "Why didn't you choose a big one?" He replied, "Since I am younger, I should eat a small one. The big ones should be kept for parents and elders." Think about this. Kong Rong was only four years old, but he already knew how to yield to others and be affectionate and filial. Endowed with such virtues, he was an extraordinary child. His good reputation has been passed down through the generations and become widely known. It is said, "Rong, at age four, could yield pears."

During the Eastern Han dynasty, there was another child named Huang Xiang. His mother died when he was nine,

，用自己的身體替父親溫暖被褥，深恐父親著涼。在夏天的時候，用扇子來扇父親的枕蓆，深恐父親太熱。這種孝心，在民間流傳不朽，所謂「香九歲，能溫蓆」。

這兩個小孩子的行爲，乃是由眞心流露出來，並不是戴假面具，來欺騙其他人。這種行爲，可以效法。你們都是兒童，要學習這兩個小孩子孝順父母的行爲，作爲規範。

你們都是幸運者，生在這個富裕的國家，生活安定，物資豐富，在這種優越環境之下，要是不好好讀書，就辜負了父母的期待、師長的希望。

在這極樂的國家，需要良善的好人，需要明理的人。要知道怎樣愛國家，怎樣做優秀的公民。你們在佛教學校讀書，將來作爲社會的模範，領導世人向善的道路邁進。以萬佛聖城六大宗旨爲標準：（一）不爭；（二）不貪；（三）不求；（四）不自私；（五）不自利；（六）不妄語。你們眞能實行這六大宗旨，將

and he was very filial to his father. In the winter, Xiang used his body heat to warm up his father's quilt, so his father wouldn't catch cold. In the summer he fanned his father's bedding, so his father wouldn't be too hot. That kind of filiality shall always be remembered. It is said, "Xiang, at age nine, warmed his father's quilt."

Those two children behaved that way spontaneously, out of sincerity; they weren't putting on an act to try to fool other people. We ought to compare our own conduct to theirs. You children should emulate those two filial children and regard them as your models.

You are all lucky to have been born in this affluent country where you can live in peace and safety and enjoy abundant resources. If you don't study hard in this excellent environment, you will disappoint the hopes of your parents and fall short of your teachers' expectations.

In this country of abundant happiness, we need good, kind, and reasonable people who know how to love their country and be good citizens. You now study in a Buddhist school, and in the future you should be role models in society, leading the people of this world to advance towards goodness. Use the Six Guidelines of the City as a standard: not fighting, not being greedy, not seeking, not being selfish, not pursuing personal advantage, and not lying. If you can truly practice these Six Guidelines, you will surely become

來一定是世界上最優秀的人。我希望你們成爲十全十美的好人，影響世人改惡向善；有大慈悲心，能給予眾生快樂，能拔眾生痛苦。人人能如此，則世界大同。

excellent people. I hope you all become completely whole-some people who can influence others to change from evil to good. I hope you will have great mercy and compassion so you can make living beings happy and alleviate their sufferings. If everyone can do this, the world will be in total harmony.

附錄
APPENDICES

辭彙解釋
GLOSSARY

索引
INDEX

法界佛教總會簡介
THE DHARMA REALM BUDDHIST ASSOCIATION

宣化上人簡傳
A BIOGRAPHICAL SKETCH OF THE
VENERABLE MASTER HSUAN HUA

宣化上人十八大願
THE EIGHTEEN GREAT VOWS OF THE
VENERABLE MASTER HSUAN HUA

宇宙白
WHITE UNIVERSE

Glossary

This glossary is to aid readers unfamiliar with the Buddhist vocabulary. Definitions have been kept simple, and are not necessarily complete.

Ajnatakaundinya, Venerable 憍陳如尊者 One of the first five Bhikshus, the first person to become enlightened to the Four Truths taught by the Buddha. His name means "first to be liberated."

Amitabha Buddha 阿彌陀佛 The Buddha of the Land of Ultimate Bliss, the Buddha of Limitless Light. Also known as Amitayus, the Buddha of Limitless Life.

Ananda, Venerable 阿難尊者 One of the ten great disciples of the Buddha Shakyamuni, Ananda was the Buddha's first cousin and his attendant. He also compiled and edited the Sutras. His name means rejoicing, because he was born on the day the Buddha realized Buddhahood. With his flawless memory, Ananda was able to remember all the Sutras the Buddha spoke and was foremost among the Buddha's disciples in erudition.

Arhat 阿羅漢 An enlightened sage of the Small Vehicle.

asuras 阿修羅 A Sanskrit term interpreted as "beings who like to fight," *asuras* are one of the eightfold division of ghosts and spirits. *Asuras* are found in the heavens, human realm, and among animals and ghosts.

birth and death 生死 The state of common, unenlightened beings, who perceive themselves as being born and dying, transmigrating endlessly in the six paths of rebirth.

Bodhi resolve 菩提心 (In Sanskrit, *bodhicitta*.) The resolve to achieve Bodhi (enlightenment) through spiritual practice. Also translated as Bodhi mind.

Bodhisattva 菩薩 An enlightened being who does not enter Nirvana but chooses instead to remain in the world and save living beings.

Bodhisattva Path 菩薩道 The path followed by those who bring forth the Bodhi resolve. The cultivation of the six *paramitas* (giving, holding precepts, patience, vigor, samadhi, and wisdom) and the myriad practices is an essential aspect of the Bodhisattva Path.

Buddha 佛 One who has achieved the ultimate, perfect enlightenment.

Buddhadharma 佛法 The methods of cultivation taught by the Buddha that lead beings to enlightenment.

Buddha-nature 佛性 The potential for Buddhahood that is inherent in all living beings. The Buddha-nature is nondual and all beings are equally endowed with it. It does not increase in an enlightened being nor is it less in a confused being.

Chan 禪 The abbreviated Chinese transliteration of the Sanskrit word *dhyana*. The general meaning of *dhyana* is meditation. The Japanese pronounce the character *chan* as 'Zen.' The Chan School is foremost among the Five Great Schools of Buddhism in that it transmits the Buddha's Mind Seal, pointing directly to the mind so that one sees one's nature and becomes a Buddha.

Confucius 孔子 The foremost sage and philosopher of China who lived in the fifth century B.C., he taught that every person should fulfill his or her proper role in family and society. His philosophy forms the basis of Chinese culture and tradition.

cultivation 修行 The practical application of the methods taught by the Buddha that lead to enlightenment. Such spiritual practice is likened to the process of cultivating a field, starting from plowing and planting and resulting in fruition, harvest, and storage.

demon 魔 From the Sanskrit *mara*, the term means "bringer of death."

dharma 法 (1) A generic term for all the various kinds of things or entities that exist in the world, including both physical and mental phenomena. (2) A method.

Dharma 法 (Also: Buddhadharma) The teachings of Buddhas.

Dharma body 法身 The embodiment of Truth; the spiritual or "true" body of the Buddha, which is universally pervasive.

Dharma assembly 法會 A gathering where the Dharma is expounded or practiced.

Dharma-door 法門 A method of practice.

Dharma-ending Age 末法時代 The last of the three ages of Dharma. After the Buddha speaks the Dharma, there follows the Proper Dharma Age, which lasts 1000 years. It is followed by the Dharma Image Age, which also lasts 1000 years. The last period is the Dharma-ending Age, the age strong in fighting, which lasts for 10,000 years. During this age, the understanding and practice of the Buddha's teachings gradually decline and finally disappear.

Dharma Flower Sutra 法華經 Also known as the *Lotus Sutra*, this is one of the most important Mahayana Sutras; spoken by the Buddha in the final stage of his teaching, it is the Sutra for the realization of Buddhahood.

Dharma Master 法師 A teacher of Dharma. A respectful term of address for members of the Sangha.

Dharma Realm 法界 (1) The enlightened world, the totality of the realm of the Buddhas. (2) A particular plane of existence, such as one of the ten Dharma Realms of Buddhist cosmology. There are four sagely Dharma Realms (those of Buddhas, Bodhisattvas, Pratyekabuddhas, and Hearers) and six common Dharma Realms (those of gods, *asuras*, humans, animals, hungry ghosts, and hell-beings).

Dharma-protecting spirits 護法神 Invisible beings who have resolved or made vows to protect the Buddha's teachings. These beings include the eightfold division of gods, dragons, *yakshas* ('speedy ghosts'), *gandharvas* (incense-inhaling spirits), *asuras* (beings who like to fight), *garudas* (great eagle-like birds), *kinnaras* (musical spirits), and *mahoragas* (great python-spirits).

Dharma-selecting vision 擇法眼 The ability to discriminate between what is proper Dharma and what is not.

Dhyana 禪 A Sanskrit word that translates as "stilling one's thoughts" and refers to meditation. *Chan* in Chinese, *zen* in Japanese.

Earth Store Bodhisattva 地藏菩薩 (In Sanskrit, Ksitigarbha Bodhisattva.) Of the four great Bodhisattvas who have special affinities with our world, Earth Store Bodhisattva is the Bodhisattva of Great Vows, known for his vow that he will not become a Buddha until the hells are empty. He specializes in saving beings from the three evil paths, especially from the hells.

evil world of five turbidities 五濁惡世 A name for the world we live in. This world has Five Turbidities, which are:
1. The Turbidity of Time, because it cannot be distinguished clearly.
2. The Turbidity of Views, because everyone has his or her own views, and it is impossible to separate them clearly from one another.
3. The Turbidity of Afflictions, because each one's afflictions can set off others' afflictions.
4. The Turbidity of Living Beings, because beings may transmigrate in the six paths.
5. The Turbidity of Life Spans, because living beings' durations are unknown and unfixed.

false thoughts 妄想 The discursive thoughts of the conscious mind, which obstruct the wisdom of our inherent nature.

filiality 孝順 Also known as filial piety, it refers to respect and appreciation for parents, teachers, and elders.

five desires 五欲 The desires for wealth, sex, fame, food, and sleep. These desires are the "roots of the hells."

Five Eyes 五眼 These five spiritual eyes, possessed by all people, will open in the process of diligent cultivation. They are the Buddha Eye, the Wisdom Eye, the Dharma Eye, the Heavenly Eye, and the Flesh Eye.

five precepts 五戒 The fundamental precepts received by laity, they are: no killing, no stealing, no sexual misconduct, no lying, and no intoxicants (including cigarettes and drugs of all kinds).

gods 天神 Gods, according to Buddhist teaching, live in various heavens. They are not immortal or omnipotent. They do have long life spans and various spiritual powers. Anyone can be reborn as a god by generating the appropriate good karma; however, gods are not enlightened. They eventually die and are reborn in lower realms according to their karma.

golden-winged *peng* birds 大鵬金翅鳥 Also known as *garudas*, they have a wingspan of about 3000 miles. When they flap their wings, the ocean waters part and all the dragons at the bottom of the sea are exposed as potential meals. The dragons are gobbled up on the spot by the *peng* birds, who eat them with the same relish as we eat noodles.

good advisors 善知識 Wise teachers with proper knowledge and views who cultivates in accord with the Buddhadharma and teach and transform others using the Four Methods of Conversion (giving, kind words, beneficial conduct, and cooperation).

Great Vehicle 大乘 This is a translation of the Sanskrit term *Mahayana* and refers to the vehicle of the Bodhisattvas that is large enough to hold and carry across all living beings. In these compassionate teachings the Buddha stressed the Bodhisattva Path of enlightening both oneself and others, saving both oneself and others.

Guanyin (Guanshiyin) Bodhisattva 觀音菩薩 (In Sanskrit, Avalokiteshvara Bodhisattva.) Of the four great Bodhisattvas who have affinities with our world, Guanshiyin or Guanyin is the Bodhisattva of Great Compassion. His name means "Contemplating the Sounds of the World."

Guanyin session 觀音七 A session, usually seven days long, during which participants recite the name of Guanyin Bodhisattva.

Hearers 聲聞 Also known as Arhats, these are the Buddha's disciples who awaken to the Way by hearing the sound of the Buddha's teachings.

inherent nature 自性 Another name for the Buddha-nature inherent in all living beings.

Jade Emperor 玉皇大帝 A deity revered within Daoism and popular Chinese religion. Also known as the God of Christianity, or as Shakra or Indra within the Hindu pantheon. He is the lord of the second heaven of the desire realm, the Heaven of the Thirty-three.

karma 業 A Sanskrit word that means "deeds," what we do. Karma can be good, evil, or neutral and is created by body, mouth, and mind.

Land of Ultimate Bliss 極樂世界 (In Sanskrit, Sukhavati.) The Buddhaland of Amitabha Buddha in the West created through the power of his forty-eight vows that enable living beings to be reborn in his land simply by sincere mindfulness and recitation of his name. Also known as the Western Pure Land.

Lao Zi 老子 A sage who lived in China around 500 B.C., his belief was in the natural course of events and he advocated "non-doing," letting things be as they are. The *Daodejing*, the principal classic of Daoism, is attributed to him.

Mencius 孟子 A Chinese philosopher and sage of the 3rd-4th centuries B.C., who is considered to have transmitted and further developed the philosophy of Confucius.

Nirvana 涅槃 A state of ultimate tranquility, perfect quiescence realized by enlightened sages.

outflows 漏 All our faults, bad habits, and afflictions that cause our vital energy to "flow out."

Pratyekabuddha (Condition-Enlightened One) 緣覺 One who attains enlightenment through contemplating the Twelve Causal Conditions (see entry).

precepts 戒 Rules of ethical conduct set forth by the Buddha to help cultivators regulate their bodies, mouths, and minds. In Buddhism, there are five precepts for laypeople, ten precepts for novices, 250 precepts for fully ordained monks and 348 precepts for fully-ordained nuns, and ten major and forty-eight minor Bodhisattva precepts for those who bring forth the Bodhisattva resolve.

Proper Dharma Age 正法時代 The first of the three ages of Dharma. See Dharma-ending Age.

Pure Land 淨土 Normally used as another name for the Western Land of Ultimate Bliss, this term can also apply to any Buddha's pure land.

Pure Land Dharma-door 淨土法門 The practice of reciting Amitabha Buddha's name as well as other practices that help one attain rebirth in the Land of Ultimate Bliss.

samadhi 定 Concentration attained through meditation and other practices. There are many types and levels of samadhi. Precepts are the basis for developing samadhi, and samadhi leads to wisdom.

Sangha 僧 The monastic order of Buddhist monks and nuns.

Sanskrit 梵文 An ancient Indian language belonging to the Indic branch of the Indo-European family of languages; the language in which the Mahayana Buddhist Sutras were preserved.

Shakyamuni Buddha 釋迦牟尼佛 The historical Buddha of this world who was born in India as Prince Siddhartha Gautama over 2500 years ago.

Shastras 論 Commentaries on the teachings of the Buddha spoken by Buddhist Patriarchs and disciples of the Buddha.

Shurangama Sutra 楞嚴經 One of the most important Mahayana Sutras in Buddhism, it will be the first Sutra to disappear in the Dharma-ending Age.

six paths of rebirth 六道輪迴 The realms where common, unenlightened beings revolve within the cycle of birth and death. These realms are those of gods, *asuras*, humans, animals, hungry ghosts, and hell-beings.

six sense faculties 六根 The eyes, ears, nose, tongue, body, and mind.

Sixth Patriarch 六祖大師 Great Master Huineng, the Sixth Buddhist Patriarch in China, whose teachings are recorded in the *Sixth Patriarch's Platform Sutra*.

Small Vehicle 小乘 The Buddha's teaching to Hearers and Pratyekabuddhas, which emphasizes enlightening and liberating oneself, but not others.

spiritual penetrations 神通 There are six spiritual penetrations: (1) the heavenly eye, (2) the heavenly ear, (3) the knowledge of others' thoughts, (4) the knowledge of past lives, (5) the complete spirit, and (6) the ending of outflows. These supernatural powers come naturally as a part of cultivation, but are not the goal of cultivation. Gods, spirits, and ghosts have attained only the first five in varying degrees.

Sutra 經 Buddhist scriptures that consist of discourses spoken by Buddhas, Bodhisattvas, or other enlightened disciples of the Buddhas.

thought-delusions 思惑 Defined as "giving rise to discriminations because one is confused about principles." There are eighty-one categories of thought delusions.

three evil paths (destinies) 三惡道 The paths/destinies of animals, hungry ghosts, and hell-beings are said to be evil, since they entail much more suffering than the good paths of gods, *asuras*, and humans.

three poisons 三毒 Greed, anger, and delusion.

Three Realms 三界 The Desire Realm, in which we live; the Form Realm, heavens free of desire that are reached through meditation and cultivation; and the Formless Realm; heavens free of desire and form that are reached through meditation and cultivation.

Three Refuges 三皈依 The formulas for taking refuge in the Triple Jewel–the Buddha, the Dharma, and the Sangha.

Tripitaka ("Three Treasuries") 三藏 The Buddhist Canon, which is divided into three divisions–Sutras, Vinaya, and Shastras.

Triple Jewel 三寶 Also called the Three Jewels or Gems, it comprises: (1) the Buddha, (2) the Dharma, and (3) the Sangha. They are Buddhism's greatest treasures. For further information, see the individual entries for each.

Triple Realm 三界 See Three Realms.

Twelve Causal Conditions 十二因緣 Those Enlightened to Conditions (Pratyekabuddhas) become enlightened by contemplating both the arising and the cessation of these twelve, which condition each other in the following sequence:
1. ignorance is the condition for activity;
2. activity is the condition for consciousness;
3. consciousness is the condition for name and form;
4. name and form are the condition for the six sense faculties;
5. the six sense faculties are the condition for contact;
6. contact is the condition for feeling;
7. feeling is the condition for emotional love;
8. emotional love is the condition for grasping;
9. grasping is the condition for becoming;
10. becoming is the condition for birth;
11. birth is the condition for
12. old age and death.

view-delusions 見惑 Defined as "giving rise to greed when confronted with things." There are eighty-eight categories of view delusions.

Vinaya 律 The collected moral regulations governing the life of the Buddhist monastic community, one of the three divisions of the Buddhist canon. The Vinaya includes all the precept-regulations, methods we use to keep watch over ourselves so that it is not necessary for anyone else to keep an eye on us.

Way 道 The spiritual path of cultivation; the ultimate truth that is realized through following that path.

Way-place 道場 (In Sanskrit, Bodhimanda.) (1) A "site of enlightenment." (2) Any place of practice–a temple, a monastery, a hermitage–regardless of its size.

Index

A

B

E

F

G

W

X

Y

法界佛教總會簡介

宗旨

法界佛教總會，前身爲中美佛教總會，創辦人——
上宣下化老和尚一九五九年創立於美國。本會以法界
爲體，以將佛教的真實義理，普遍傳播到世界各地
；以翻譯經典、弘揚正法、提倡道德教育、利樂有
情爲己任。俾使個人、家庭、社會、國家，乃至世
界，皆能蒙受佛法的薰習，而漸趨至真、至善、至
美的境地。

創辦人簡介

上人，名安慈，字度輪，接虛雲老和尚法，嗣潙仰
，法號宣化。籍東北，誕於清末民初。年十九出家
，盧墓守孝。修禪定，習教觀，日一食，夜不臥。
一九四八年抵香港，成立佛教講堂等道場。一九六
二年攜正法西來，在美開演大乘經典數十部。歷年
來，除建立法界佛教總會及所隸屬萬佛聖城等正法
道場二十多處外，並創辦譯經、教育等機構，法化

The Dharma Realm
Buddhist Association

Mission

The Dharma Realm Buddhist Association (formerly the Sino-American Buddhist Association) was founded by the Venerable Master Hsuan Hua in the United States of America in 1959. Taking the Dharma Realm as its scope, the Association aims to disseminate the genuine teachings of the Buddha throughout the world. The Association is dedicated to translating the Buddhist canon, propagating the Orthodox Dharma, promoting ethical education, and bringing benefit and happiness to all beings. Its hope is that individuals, families, the society, the nation, and the entire world will, under the transforming influence of the Buddhadharma, gradually reach the state of ultimate truth and goodness.

The Founder

The Venerable Master, whose names were An Tse and To Lun, received the Dharma name Hsuan Hua and the transmission of Dharma from Venerable Master Hsu Yun in the lineage of the Wei Yang Sect. He was born in Manchuria, China, at the beginning of the century. At nineteen, he entered the monastic order and dwelt in a hut by his mother's grave to practice filial piety. He meditated, studied the teachings, ate only one meal a day, and slept sitting up. In 1948 he went to Hong Kong, where he established the Buddhist Lecture Hall and other Way-places. In 1962 he brought the Proper Dharma to the West, lecturing on several dozen Mahayana Sutras in the United States. Over the years, the Master established more than twenty monasteries of Proper Dharma under the auspices of the Dharma Realm

東西方。一九九五年，上人示寂於美，而其一生大公無私，悲智雙運教化眾生的精神與德行，已感召無數人改過自新，走向清淨高尚的菩提大道。

弘法、譯經、教育

宣公上人一生之三大願：一、弘法。二、譯經。三、教育。為實現此三大願，上人本著三大宗旨、六大條款，不畏一切艱辛困苦，在西方建立道場，接引眾生，廣行教化。數十年來創辦的機構如下：

萬佛聖城、分支道場

為了弘揚正法，上人除了培育訓練人才之外，更致力於道場的建立，以期轉法輪，度眾生，提供修行人遵循佛制的清淨修持道場。歷年來分別成立正法道場多處，美加地區計有萬佛聖城、金山聖寺、金聖寺、金輪聖寺、金峰聖寺、金佛聖寺、華嚴聖寺、長堤聖寺、法界聖城、柏克萊寺、華嚴精舍、福祿壽聖寺等；臺灣地區則有法界佛教印經會、法界聖寺、彌陀聖寺；馬來西亞地區為紫雲洞、登彼岸

Buddhist Association and the City of Ten Thousand Buddhas. He also founded centers for the translation of the Buddhist canon and for education to spread the influence of the Dharma in the East and West. The Master manifested the stillness in the United States in 1995. Through his lifelong, selfless dedication to teaching living beings with wisdom and compassion, he influenced countless people to change their faults and to walk upon the pure, bright path to enlightenment.

Dharma Propagation, Buddhist Text Translation, and Education

The Venerable Master Hua's three great vows after leaving the home-life were (1) to propagate the Dharma, (2) to translate the Buddhist Canon, and (3) to promote education. In order to make these vows a reality, the Venerable Master based himself on the Three Principles and the Six Guidelines. Courageously facing every hardship, he founded monasteries, schools, and centers in the West, drawing in living beings and teaching them on a vast scale. Over the years, he founded the following institutions:

The City of Ten Thousand Buddhas and Its Branches

In propagating the Proper Dharma, the Venerable Master not only trained people but also founded Way-places where the Dharma wheel could turn and living beings could be saved. He wanted to provide cultivators with pure places to practice in accord with the Buddha's regulations. Over the years, he founded many Way-places of Proper Dharma. In the United States and Canada, these include the City of Ten Thousand Buddhas; Gold Mountain Monastery; Gold Sage Monastery; Gold Wheel Monastery; Gold Summit Monastery; Gold Buddha Monastery; Avatamsaka Monastery; Long Beach Monastery; the City of the Dharma Realm;

，蓮華精舍等道場；香港地區道場則是佛教講堂、
慈興寺等。

萬佛聖城購於一九七四年，爲法界佛教總會樞紐，
位於舊金山以北一百一十英哩的曼第仙諾縣達摩鎮
內。佔地四百八十八英畝，已開闢使用的場地約八
十英畝；其餘爲草原、果園及樹林。城中有七十餘
座大型建築物，大小房間二千餘間，清幽寧靜，空
氣清新，是美國第一座大型的佛教道場，也是國際
性的正法道場。

宣公上人雖爲禪宗潙仰派第九代傳人，但所屬道場
一切作息、法會與修持，均兼顧禪、淨、密、律、
教五宗的修持法門，一律平等重視，正契合佛陀所
説的「是法平等，無有高下」。道場內清規嚴謹，
住眾皆須嚴以律己，勤奮不懈，以正法爲依歸，過
著清淨無染、大公無私、身心安樂的生活；日日講
經説法，轉法輪，奉獻身心，爲復興佛教而努力。
所有的道場除了遵守佛制：「日中一食、衣不離體
」外，並遵守三大宗旨：

Berkeley Buddhist Monastery; Avatamsaka Hermitage; and Blessings, Prosperity, and Longevity Monastery. In Taiwan, there are the Dharma Realm Buddhist Books Distribution Association, Dharma Realm Monastery, and Amitabha Monastery. In Malaysia, there are Zi Yun Dong Monastery, Deng Bi An Monastery, and Lotus Vihara. In Hong Kong, there are the Buddhist Lecture Hall and Cixing Monastery.

Purchased in 1974, the City of Ten Thousand Buddhas is the hub of the Dharma Realm Buddhist Association. The City is located in Talmage, Mendocino County, California, 110 miles north of San Francisco. Eighty of the 488 acres of land are in active use. The remaining acreage consists of meadows, orchards, and woods. With over seventy large buildings containing over 2,000 rooms, blessed with serenity and fresh, clean air, it is the first large Buddhist monastic community in the United States. It is also an international center for the Proper Dharma.

Although the Venerable Master Hua was the Ninth Patriarch in the Weiyang Sect of the Chan School, the monasteries he founded emphasize all of the five main practices of Mahayana Buddhism (Chan meditation, Pure Land, esoteric, Vinaya (moral discipline), and doctrinal studies). This accords with the Buddha's words: "The Dharma is level and equal, with no high or low." At the City of Ten Thousand Buddhas, the rules of purity are rigorously observed. Residents of the City strive to regulate their own conduct and to cultivate with vigor. Taking refuge in the Proper Dharma, they lead pure and selfless lives, and attain peace in body and mind. The Sutras are expounded and the Dharma wheel is turned daily. Residents dedicate themselves wholeheartedly to making Buddhism flourish. Monks and nuns in all the monasteries take one meal a day, always wear their precept sash, and follow the Three Principles:

245

凍死不攀緣，

餓死不化緣，

窮死不求緣；

隨緣不變，不變隨緣，

抱定我們三大宗旨。

捨命爲佛事，

造命爲本事，

正命爲僧事；

即事明理，明理即事，

推行祖師一脈心傳。

六大條款：不爭、不貪、不求、不自私、不自利、不打妄語。

國際譯經學院

上人發願將三藏十二部皆譯成西方文字語言，流通全世界。故於一九七三年，在三藩市成立國際譯經學院，翻譯佛經爲英文及其他語言。該院於一九七七年，合併於法界佛教大學內，成爲譯經學院。於一九九一年，上人於柏林根市購下一棟大樓，爲國

Freezing, we do not scheme.
Starving, we do not beg.
Dying of poverty, we ask for nothing.
According with conditions, we do not change.
Not changing, we accord with conditions.
We adhere firmly to our three great principles.
We renounce our lives to do the Buddha's work.
We take the responsibility to mold our own destinies.
We rectify our lives to fulfill the Sanghan's role.
Encountering specific matters,
   we understand the principles.
Understanding the principles,
   we apply them in specific matters.
We carry on the single pulse of
   the Patriarchs' mind-transmission.

The monasteries also follow the Six Guidelines: not contending, not being greedy, not seeking, not being selfish, not pursuing personal advantage, and not lying.

International Translation Institute

The Venerable Master vowed to translate the Buddhist Canon (Tripitaka) into Western languages so that it would be widely accessible throughout the world. In 1973, he founded the International Translation Institute on Washington Street in San Francisco for the purpose of translating Buddhist scriptures into English and other languages. In 1977, the Institute was merged into Dharma Realm Buddhist University as the Institute for the Translation of Buddhist Texts. In 1991, the Venerable Master purchased a large building in Burlingame (south of San Francisco) and established the International Translation Institute there for the purpose of translating and publishing Buddhist texts. To date, in addition to publishing over one

際譯經學院永久院址，旨在翻譯經典及出版佛書。歷年來，除了已發行中文版佛經、佛書一百多冊外，另有英文版、法文版、西班牙文版、越南文版、日文版、中英版等百多冊譯本。

此外，錄音帶、錄影帶亦相續出版中。發行近卅年的金剛菩提海月刊，近幾年來更以中英雙語對照版方式刊出。譯經這項龐大艱鉅的工作，中國過去皆由國王、皇帝主辦、支持，今日上人鼓勵弟子們共同努力挑起此重責大任，藉著書籍及有聲的出版工作，運用語言文字，轉正法輪，作大佛事。凡一切有心參與此神聖工作者，均應謹守譯經學院的八項基本守則：

一、不得抱有個人的名利。

二、不得貢高我慢，必須以虔誠恭敬的態度來工作。

三、不得自讚毀他。

四、不得自以為是，對他人作品吹毛求疵。

五、以佛心為己心。

六、運用擇法眼來辨別正確的道理。

hundred volumes of Buddhist texts in Chinese, the Association has published more than one hundred volumes of English, French, Spanish, Vietnamese, and Japanese translations of Buddhist texts, as well as bilingual (Chinese and English) editions. Audio and video tapes also continue to be produced. The monthly journal *Vajra Bodhi Sea*, which has been in circulation for nearly thirty years, has been published in bilingual (Chinese and English) format in recent years.

In the past, the difficult and vast mission of translating the Buddhist canon in China was sponsored and supported by the emperors and kings themselves. In our time, the Venerable Master encouraged his disciples to cooperatively shoulder this heavy responsibility, producing books and audio tapes and using the medium of language to turn the wheel of Proper Dharma and do the great work of the Buddha. All those who aspire to devote themselves to this work of sages should uphold the Eight Guidelines of the International Translation Institute:

1. One must free oneself from the motives of personal fame and profit.

2. One must cultivate a respectful and sincere attitude free from arrogance and conceit.

3. One must refrain from aggrandizing one's work and denigrating that of others.

4. One must not establish oneself as the standard of correctness and suppress the work of others with one's fault-finding.

5. One must take the Buddha-mind as one's own mind.

6. One must use the wisdom of Dharma-Selecting Vision to determine true principles.

七、懇請十方大德長老印證其翻譯。

八、作品在獲得印證之後，必須努力弘揚流
　　通經、律、論以及佛書，以光大佛教。

這是上人的大願，亦是所有從事譯經工作者努力邁
進的目標。

育良小學、培德中學、法界佛教大學

「教育，就是最根本的國防。」宣公上人鑑於要拯
救世界，當務之急便是辦好教育；因為想救世界，
就要改造人心，使之去惡向善。故於一九七四年，
成立育良小學；一九七六年，成立培德中學及法界
佛教大學。

在融入佛教精神的教育下，小學以「孝」，中學以
「忠」，大學則以「仁義」等道德為宗旨。育良小
學、培德中學的課程，融合現代、傳統及東西文化
的優點，注重道德、精神的薰習。旨在培育出品格
高尚的世界棟樑之才，以利益世界人類。學校採中
英雙語教育，男女分校。學生們在校除接受一般美
國中小學所必須學習的科目外，並有倫理課、打坐

7. One must request Virtuous Elders of the ten directions to certify one's translations.
8. One must endeavor to propagate the teachings by printing Sutras, Shastra texts, and Vinaya texts when the translations are certified as being correct.

These are the Venerable Master's vows, and participants in the work of translation should strive to realize them.

Instilling Goodness Elementary School, Developing Virtue Secondary School, Dharma Realm Buddhist University

"Education is the best national defense." The Venerable Master Hua saw clearly that in order to save the world, it is essential to promote good education. If we want to save the world, we have to bring about a complete change in people's minds and guide them to cast out unwholesomeness and to pursue goodness. To this end the Master founded Instilling Goodness Elementary School in 1974, and Developing Virtue Secondary School and Dharma Realm Buddhist University in 1976.

In an education embodying the spirit of Buddhism, the elementary school teaches students to be filial to parents, the secondary school teaches students to be good citizens, and the university teaches such virtues as humaneness and righteousness. Instilling Goodness Elementary School and Developing Virtue Secondary School combine the best of contemporary and traditional methods and of Western and Eastern cultures. They emphasize moral virtue and spiritual development, and aim to guide students to become good and capable citizens who will benefit humankind. The schools offer

251

課、佛學課等，以奠定學生良好的道德基礎，逐步引導學生認識自我、探索宇宙的真理。除了萬佛聖城之外，各道場亦設有育良小學、培德中學分校（週日班），將孝道及倫理道德等教育，普遍推行於各地。

以正法為教學主要內容的法界佛教大學，不僅傳授專業知識，更注重以倫理道德為基礎，擴展至幫助所有人類、一切眾生回歸自性的研習。故法界大學提倡共同研究、自由交換理念的風氣，鼓勵學生修學各種經典，以不同的經驗及學習層面，推動主觀智能，來發揮經典的意趣妙理；同時注重實際修持，使佛法與生活融合為一，滋養慧命，充實德行，從中造就出品行高潔、出類拔萃的優秀人才，以利益群生。

僧伽居士訓練班

有鑑於末法時代，東西方社會普遍缺乏真實依佛制行持、戒律精嚴的道場，以及具真知灼見的明眼善知識，來引導有意從事佛教事業的人士。又為了提高僧眾素質，令正法久住，造就行解並進的國際佛

a bilingual (Chinese/English) program where boys and girls study separately. In addition to standard academic courses, the curriculum includes ethics, meditation, Buddhist studies, and so on, giving students a foundation in virtue and guiding them to understand themselves and explore the truths of the universe. Branches of the schools (Sunday schools) have been established at branch monasteries with the aim of propagating filial piety and ethical education.

Dharma Realm Buddhist University, whose curriculum focuses on the Proper Dharma, does not merely transmit academic knowledge. It emphasizes a foundation in virtue, which expands into the study of how to help all living beings discover their inherent nature. Thus, Dharma Realm Buddhist University advocates a spirit of shared inquiry and free exchange of ideas, encouraging students to study various canonical texts and use different experiences and learning styles to tap their inherent wisdom and fathom the meanings of those texts. Students are encouraged to practice the principles they have understood and apply the Buddhadharma in their lives, thereby nurturing their wisdom and virtue. The University aims to produce outstanding individuals of high moral character who will be able to bring benefit to all sentient beings.

Sangha and Laity Training Programs
In the Dharma-ending Age, in both Eastern and Western societies there are very few monasteries that actually practice the Buddha's regulations and strictly uphold the precepts. Teachers with genuine wisdom and understanding, capable of guiding those who aspire to pursue careers in Buddhism, are very rare. The Venerable Master founded the Sangha and Laity Training Programs in 1982 with the goals of raising the caliber of the Sangha, perpetuating the Proper Dharma, providing

教人才，以續佛慧命。因此，上人於一九八二年成立僧伽居士訓練班。

僧伽訓練班爲令出家眾在佛學修習方面，能奠定良好穩固的基礎，不但訓練僧眾實際參與佛教事務，建立僧團職事概念，以期畢業後，在各道場、寺廟，及其他環境中，擔任佛教的種種職務。又特別注重學生們充實佛教教理，深入經藏；認眞修行，嚴持戒律，培養高尚德行，以弘揚正法，續佛慧命。居士訓練班亦予居士適當的課程，使學生們具正知正見，修持佛法、研究教理，齊頭並進，了解寺院的種種規矩與禮儀，以期於佛教團體生活中發揮所能，服務人群。

齊心共進

時值末法，世風險惡，本著法界佛教總會的宗旨，本會所屬之道場、機構，皆門戶開放，沒有人我、宗教、國籍等分別。凡願致力於仁義道德，追求眞理，明心見性，利益人類的人士，皆歡迎至此，齊心努力研究，踏實修持學習，大家共同爲利樂眾生而努力。

professional training for Buddhists around the world on both practical and theoretical levels, and transmitting the wisdom of the Buddha.

The Sangha Training Program gives monastics a solid foundation in Buddhist studies and practice, training them in the practical affairs of Buddhism and Sangha management. After graduation, students will be able to assume various responsibilities related to Buddhism in monasteries, institutions, and other settings. The program emphasizes a thorough knowledge of Buddhism, understanding of the scriptures, earnest cultivation, strict observance of precepts, and the development of a virtuous character, so that students will be able to propagate the Proper Dharma and perpetuate the Buddha's wisdom. The Laity Training Program offers courses to help laypeople develop correct views, study and practice the teachings, and understand monastic regulations and ceremonies, so that they will be able to contribute their abilities in Buddhist organizations.

Let Us Go Forward Together

In this Dharma-ending Age when the world is becoming increasingly dangerous and evil, the Dharma Realm Buddhist Association, in consonance with its guiding principles, opens the doors of its monasteries and centers to those of all religions and nationalities. Anyone who is devoted to humaneness, righteousness, virtue, and the pursuit of truth, and who wishes to understand him or herself and help humankind, is welcome to come study and practice with us. May we together bring benefit and happiness to all living beings.

宣化上人簡傳

東北時期

宣公上人，東北吉林省雙城縣人，民初戊午年農曆三月十六日生。俗姓白，名玉書，又名玉禧。父富海公，一生勤儉治家，以務農為業。母胡太夫人，生前茹素念佛，數十年如一日；懷上人時，曾向佛菩薩祈願，生上人前夕，夢見阿彌陀佛大放光明，遂生上人。

上人生性沉默寡言，天賦俠義心腸，幼年即隨母親茹素念佛。年十一，見鄰居一死嬰，感生死事大，無常迅速，毅然有出家之志。十二歲，聞雙城王孝子 上常 下仁大師，盡孝得道，發願效法。懺悔過去不孝父母，決定每日早晚向父母叩頭認錯，以報親恩，自此漸以孝行見稱，人稱「白孝子」。

十五歲皈依 上常 下智老和尚為師。同年入學，於四書五經、諸子百家、醫卜星相等，無不貫通。求學

A Biographical Sketch of the Venerable Master Hsuan Hua

Early Years in Manchuria

The Venerable Master was born in Shuangcheng County, Jilin Province, China, on the sixteenth day of the third lunar month in the year of *wuwu* at the beginning of the century. He was named Yushu (or Yuxi) Bai. His father, Fuhai Bai, was a hardworking, frugal farmer. His mother, whose maiden name was Hu, was vegetarian and recited the Buddha's name all her life. While carrying the Master, she prayed to the Buddhas and Bodhisattvas. The night before his birth, she saw Amitabha Buddha emitting brilliant light in her dream. Following that, the Master was born.

As a child, the Master was taciturn, but had a heroic spirit. He followed his mother in being vegetarian and reciting the Buddha's name. At the age of eleven, the sight of a dead infant made him aware of the great matter of birth and death, and he resolved to leave the home-life. At twelve, he heard of the filial practice of Filial Son Wang (Great Master Chang Ren) of Shuangcheng County and vowed to emulate him. The Master repented for not having been a good son and began to bow to his parents every morning and evening to repay their kindness. Because of his filial piety, he became known as Filial Son Bai.

At fifteen, he took refuge with the Venerable Master Chang Zhi. He also started school and mastered the Four Books, the Five Classics, the texts of various Chinese philosophers, and the fields of medicine, divination, astrology, and physiognomy. He

期間，參加道德會等慈善團體；又爲不識字者，講
《六祖壇經》、《金剛經》等；爲貧寒者，創辦義
務學校。

十九歲母親逝世，遂禮請三緣寺^上常^下智老和尚爲剃
度，法名安慈，字度輪。並披緇結廬於母親墓旁，
守孝期間，發十八大願，拜華嚴、禮淨懺、修禪定
、習教觀、日一食、夜不臥，功夫日純，得鄉里人
民之愛戴禮敬，其洗鍊精虔，感動諸佛菩薩、護法
龍天，故靈異之事多不勝數，人稱奇僧。

一日打坐，見六祖大師至茅棚，告曰：「將來你會
到西方，所遇之人無量無邊，教化眾生，如恆河沙
，不可悉數，此是西方佛法崛起之徵象。」言畢，
忽而不見。守孝期滿，隱居於長白山支脈彌陀洞內
修苦行。後回三緣寺，爲首座。居東北期間，觀機
逗教，點化迷蒙，濟世活人，感化無量龍蛇、狐狸
、鬼神，求皈受戒，改惡修善。

一九四六年，慕虛雲老和尚爲宗門泰斗，遂束裝就
道，前往參禮。途中備經艱苦，蹤跡遍及內陸各大

was active in the Virtue Society and other charity groups. He explained the *Sixth Patriarch's Sutra*, the *Vajra Sutra*, and other Sutras for the illiterate and started a free school for the poor.

At nineteen, after his mother's death, he requested Venerable Master Chang Zhi of Sanyuan (Three Conditions) Monastery to shave his head. He was given the Dharma names An Tse and To Lun. Donning monk's robes, he built a simple hut by his mother's grave and lived there for three years in observance of filial piety. During that period, he made eighteen great vows. He bowed to the *Flower Adornment Sutra*, repented and meditated, studied scriptures, ate only one meal a day, and slept sitting up at night. His skill in cultivation won the admiration of the villagers and evoked miraculous responses from the Buddhas, Bodhisattvas, and Dharma-protecting gods and dragons. He was regarded as an extraordinary monk.

One day while meditating, he saw the Sixth Patriarch come to his hut and tell him, "In the future you will go to the West and meet countless people. You will teach and transform beings as countless as the sands of the Ganges River. That will mark the beginning of the Buddhadharma in the West." With those words, the Sixth Patriarch vanished. The Master completed his filial observance and went to Changbai Mountain, where he dwelt in seclusion and practiced austerities at the Amitabha Cave. Later, he returned to Sanyuan Monastery and was made the head of the assembly. During his years in Manchuria, the Master taught people according to their potentials. He awakened those who were confused and saved many lives. Countless dragons, snakes, foxes, ghosts, and spirits reformed themselves upon receiving the refuges and precepts from him.

In 1946, the Master embarked on an arduous journey to pay homage to greatly revered Elder Master Hsu Yun. Along the

梵剎，一九四七年赴普陀山受具足戒，一九四八年抵廣州曹溪南華寺，禮虛雲老和尚，受命任南華寺戒律學院監學，後轉任教務主任。雲公觀其爲法門龍象，乃傳授法脈，賜法號宣化，遂爲潙仰宗第九代接法人，摩訶迦葉初祖傳承之第四十五代。

香江演教

一九四九年，叩別虛雲老和尚，赴香港弘法，闡揚禪、教、律、密、淨五宗並重，打破門户之見。並重建古刹、印經造像，成立西樂園寺、慈興禪寺、佛教講堂。居港十餘年間，應眾生懇請，普結法緣，相續開講大乘經典多部，舉辦佛七、禪七、拜懺等法會，又創辦《心法》雜誌等，終日爲弘揚大法而奔忙，使佛法興於香江。其間亦曾數度赴泰國、緬甸等地，考察南傳佛教，志欲溝通大小乘，以團結佛教力量。

大法西傳

一九五九年，師觀察西方機緣成熟，爲將佛教之眞實義理傳播至世界各地，遂令弟子在美成立中美佛

way, he stayed at various renowned monasteries and received complete ordination at Mount Putuo in 1947. Arriving at Nanhua Monastery in Caoxi, Guangzhou, in 1948, he paid homage to Elder Master Hsu Yun. The Elder Master made him an instructor and later the Dean of Academic Affairs at Nanhua Vinaya Academy. He saw that the Master was an outstanding individual and transmitted the Dharma to him, giving him the Dharma name Hsuan Hua and making him the Ninth Patriarch of the Weiyang Sect, in the forty-fifth generation since the First Patriarch Mahakashyapa.

Teaching in Hong Kong

In 1949, the Master bid farewell to the Elder Master Yun and went to Hong Kong. In propagating the Dharma there, he emphasized all five schools of Buddhism (Chan, Doctrine, Vinaya, Esoteric, and Pure Land) and abolished sectarianism. He renovated old temples, printed Sutras, and constructed images. He founded Western Bliss Gardens Monastery, Cixing Chan Monastery, and the Buddhist Lecture Hall. For more than ten years, he created extensive Dharma-affinities with the people of Hong Kong. He expounded various Mahayana Sutras, organized recitation, meditation, and repentance sessions, and published the magazine *Hsin Fa (Mind Dharma)*. As a result of his energetic efforts, Buddhism flourished in Hong Kong. He also visited other countries such as Thailand and Burma to study Theravada Buddhism, in the hope of bringing the Mahayana and Theravada traditions together and uniting the forces of Buddhism.

The Dharma Goes West

In 1959, the Master saw that conditions were ripe in the West. For the sake of propagating Buddhism throughout the world,

教總會（法界佛教總會前身）。一九六一年，赴澳洲弘法一年，以機緣未熟，一九六二年返港。同年應美國佛教人士邀請，隻身赴美，樹正法幢於三藩市佛教講堂。初住無窗之潮濕地窖，猶如墳墓，故自號「墓中僧」。時值美蘇兩國有古巴飛彈危機之事，為求戰爭不起，世界和平，故絕食五星期。絕食畢，危機遂解。

一九六八年，成立暑假楞嚴講修班，有華盛頓州州立大學學生三十餘人，遠來學習佛法。結業後，美籍青年五人，懇求剃度出家，創美國佛教史始有僧相之記錄。隨著日益擴大的僧團，原有的佛教講堂不足敷用，遂於一九七○年成立金山禪寺。一九七六年購置國際性大道場萬佛聖城。爾後金輪聖寺、金峰聖寺、華嚴聖寺、金佛聖寺、法界聖城等各分支道場相繼成立。上人不遺餘力致力於弘法、譯經、教育等事業，廣建道場、培植人才、訂立宗旨。集四眾之真誠，盡未來際劫，遍虛空法界，光大如來正法家業。

在弘法方面，上人教導弟子天天參禪打坐、念佛、

he instructed his disciples to establish the Sino-American Buddhist Association (renamed the Dharma Realm Buddhist Association) in the United States. In 1961 he propagated the Dharma in Australia for one year. Since the conditions were not ripe there, he returned to Hong Kong in 1962. Later that year, at the invitation of Buddhists in America, the Master traveled alone to the United States and raised the banner of the Proper Dharma at the Buddhist Lecture Hall in San Francisco. Living in a damp, windowless basement that resembled a grave, he called himself "The Monk in the Grave." During the Cuban Missile Crisis, the Master observed a five-week fast to pray for peace. By the end of his fast, the crisis was over.

During the Shurangama Study and Practice Summer Session in 1968, over thirty students from the University of Washington in Seattle went to San Francisco to study with the Master. At the end of the session, five of them requested permission to enter the monastic life. That was the beginning of the Sangha in the history of American Buddhism. The Buddhist Lecture Hall became too small for the growing Sangha. Gold Mountain Dhyana Monastery was founded in 1970, and the City of Ten Thousand Buddhas was established in 1976 as an international monastic community. Later various branches were founded, such as Gold Wheel Monastery, Gold Summit Monastery, Avatamsaka Monastery, Gold Buddha Monastery, and the City of the Dharma Realm. The Master devoted himself to the propagation of the Dharma, the translation of the Buddhist Canon, and education. He established monasteries, helped people develop their talents, and set forth principles. He led the fourfold assembly in working to spread Proper Dharma throughout the Dharma Realm.

The Master taught his disciples to meditate, recite the Buddha's name, practice repentance, study the Sutras, and observe the

263

拜懺、研究經典、嚴持戒律、日中一食、衣不離體，和合共住，互相砥礪，在西方建立行持正法之僧團，以圖匡扶正教，令正法久住。又開放萬佛聖城爲國際性宗教中心，提倡融合南北傳佛教，團結世界宗教，大家互相學習，溝通合作，共同追求眞理，爲世界和平而努力。

「只要我有一口氣在，就要講經說法。」上人講經說法，深入淺出，數十年如一日。並極力栽培四眾弘法人才，觀機逗教，化導東西方善信。多次率團至各大學，及世界各國弘法訪問，以期引導眾生改惡向善，開啓本有智慧。

在譯經方面，現已有百餘本譯爲英文，中英文雙語佛書也陸續在出版中。另有西班牙文、越南文、日文等譯本，法文、德文譯本則指日可待。預計將《大藏經》譯成各國文字，使佛法傳遍寰宇。近三十年歷史的《金剛菩提海》雜誌先是純英文版，後逐漸演變爲中英對照月刊，今共發行了三百多期。至於中文佛書更是接踵而出，不下百部，多種語言之

precepts. He taught them to eat only one meal a day (at midday) and to always wear the precept sash. He taught them to dwell in harmony and to encourage each other. He established a Sangha that practices the Proper Dharma in the West, in the hope of restoring orthodox Buddhism and keeping it alive in the world forever. The Master founded the City of Ten Thousand Buddhas as an international spiritual community where followers of different traditions of Buddhism and religions of the world can come together to learn, communicate, and work together for the sake of truth and world peace.

"As long as I have a single breath left, I will explain the Sutras and speak the Dharma." The Master expounded the Sutras and Dharma daily for several decades, explaining profound principles in a way that made them easy to understand. He also trained his monastic and lay disciples to explain the teachings. Always adjusting his teaching to the individual and the situation, he transformed both Eastern and Western disciples. He led numerous delegations to teach the Dharma in universities and nations around the world, inspiring people to turn toward goodness and discover their innate wisdom.

To date, over a hundred volumes of the Master's explanations of the scriptures have been translated into English, and some have been published in bilingual Chinese/English format. A number of Spanish, Vietnamese, and Japanese translations have been published, and French and German versions will soon be available. The Master's aim is to translate the entire Buddhist Canon into all languages so that the Dharma will be readily accessible worldwide. The monthly journal *Vajra Bodhi Sea* was first published nearly thirty years ago in English only. Later it adopted a bilingual Chinese/English format, and to date over 300 issues have been published. Over a hundred Chinese Buddhist texts have also been published. Audio and video tapes

錄音帶、錄影帶亦不斷發行中，以爲眾生聞法修行
之良箴。

在教育方面，萬佛聖城設有育良小學、培德中學、
法界佛教大學、僧伽居士訓練班等教育機構。分支
道場於周末、周日亦附設佛學班、中文學校。這些
融入佛教精神的教育機構以孝悌忠信、禮義廉恥八
德，爲做人的基礎。以大公無私、慈悲喜捨爲究竟
目標。男女分校，提倡義務教學，培養品格高尚、
具備眞知灼見的人才，以期利益世界人類。

法輪無盡

上人一生大公無私，發願代眾生受一切苦難，將己
身一切福樂迴向法界眾生，難行能行，難忍能忍，
其堅貞之志節，堪爲疾風中之勁燭，烈火內之精金
。上人曾撰一聯以明其志：

> 凍死不攀緣，
> 餓死不化緣，
> 窮死不求緣；
> 隨緣不變，不變隨緣，
> 抱定我們三大宗旨。

in several languages are currently being produced, so that people may hear the Dharma and cultivate accordingly.

In the area of education, the Master established Instilling Goodness Elementary School, Developing Virtue Secondary School, Dharma Realm Buddhist University, and the Sangha and Laity Training Programs at the City of Ten Thousand Buddhas. Many of the branch monasteries of the Dharma Realm Buddhist Association have weekend classes in Buddhism and Chinese for children as well. These educational programs integrate the teachings of Buddhism with the eight virtues of filiality, fraternal respect, loyalty, trustworthiness, propriety, righteousness, incorruptibility, and a sense of shame. Their ultimate aim is to encourage students to develop a public-minded spirit, kindness, compassion, joy, and charity. Boys and girls study separately, and the faculty of volunteer teachers guides students to develop into capable individuals with integrity and wisdom who will be able to benefit humankind.

The Infinite Dharma Wheel

The Master's life was one of total selflessness. He vowed to take the suffering and hardships of all living beings upon himself, and to dedicate to them all the blessings and happiness that he himself ought to enjoy. He practiced what was difficult to practice and endured what was difficult to endure. No amount of hardship could deter him from fulfilling his lofty resolves. He composed a verse expressing his principles:

> Freezing, we do not scheme.
> Starving, we do not beg.
> Dying of poverty, we ask for nothing.
> According with conditions, we do not change.
> Not changing, we accord with conditions.
> We adhere firmly to our three great principles.

捨命爲佛事，

造命爲本事，

正命爲僧事；

即事明理，明理即事，

推行祖師一脈心傳。

上人又堅守一生奉行之六大條款：「不爭、不貪、不求、不自私、不自利、不打妄語」，利益群生；其慈悲智慧之教化，捨己爲人、以身作則之精神，令無數人眞誠改過，走向清淨光明之菩提大道。

眾生障深福薄，一九九五年一代聖人遽爾示寂，娑婆眾生頓失依怙；然而上人之一生，即是一部法界的華嚴大經，雖示現涅槃，而恒轉無盡法輪不留痕跡，從虛空來，回到虛空去。弟子眾等唯有恪遵師教，抱定宗旨，在菩薩道上精進不懈，以期報上人浩瀚之深恩於萬一。

We renounce our lives to do the Buddha's work.
We take the responsibility to mold our own destinies.
We rectify our lives to fulfill the Sanghan's role.
Encountering specific matters,
  we understand the principles.
Understanding the principles,
  we apply them in specific matters.
We carry on the single pulse of
  the Patriarchs' mind-transmission.

Through his unwavering, lifelong maintenance of the six guiding principles of not contending, not being greedy, not seeking, not being selfish, not pursuing personal advantage, and not lying, he brought benefit to many. Teaching with wisdom and compassion, dedicating himself to serving others, and acting as a model for others, he influenced countless people to change their faults and to walk upon the pure, bright path to enlightenment.

Deep are the obstructions of living beings and scanty are their blessings, for this Sage manifested entry into stillness in 1995 and we of the Saha World suddenly lost our refuge. Yet the Venerable Master's life is actually an enactment of the great Sutra of the Dharma Realm—the *Flower Adornment Sutra*. Although he has manifested entry into Nirvana, he constantly turns the infinite Dharma wheel. He came from space, and to space he returned without leaving a trace. His disciples must carefully follow their teacher's instructions, hold fast to their principles, honor the Buddha's regulations, and advance with vigor toward Bodhi so that they may repay a tiny fraction of the Venerable Master's boundless and profound grace.

宣化上人十八大願

一、願盡虛空、遍法界、十方三世一切菩薩等，若有一未成佛時，我誓不取正覺。

二、願盡虛空、遍法界、十方三世一切緣覺等，若有一未成佛時，我誓不取正覺。

三、願盡虛空、遍法界、十方三世一切聲聞等，若有一未成佛時，我誓不取正覺。

四、願三界諸天人等，若有一未成佛時，我誓不取正覺。

五、願十方世界一切人等，若有一未成佛時，我誓不取正覺。

270

The Eighteen Great Vows of Venerable Master Hsuan Hua

1. I vow that as long as there is a single Bodhisattva in the three periods of time throughout the ten directions of the Dharma Realm, to the very ends of empty space, who has not accomplished Buddhahood, I too will not attain the right enlightenment.

2. I vow that as long as there is a single Pratyekabuddha in the three periods of time throughout the ten directions of the Dharma Realm, to the very ends of empty space, who has not accomplished Buddhahood, I too will not attain the right enlightenment.

3. I vow that as long as there is a single Shravaka in the three periods of time throughout the ten directions of the Dharma Realm, to the very ends of empty space, who has not accomplished Buddhahood, I too will not attain the right enlightenment.

4. I vow that as long as there is a single god in the Triple Realm who has not accomplished Buddhahood, I too will not attain the right enlightenment.

5. I vow that as long as there is a single human being in the worlds of the ten directions who has not accomplished Buddhahood, I too will not attain the right enlightenment.

六、願天、人、一切阿修羅等，若有一未成佛時，
　　我誓不取正覺。

七、願一切畜生界等，若有一未成佛時，我誓不取
　　正覺。

八、願一切餓鬼界等，若有一未成佛時，我誓不取
　　正覺。

九、願一切地獄界等，若有一未成佛，或地獄不空
　　時，我誓不取正覺。

十、願凡是三界諸天、仙、人、阿修羅，飛潛動植
　　、靈界龍畜、鬼神等眾，曾經皈依我者，若有
　　一未成佛時，我誓不取正覺。

十一、願將我所應享受一切福樂，悉皆迴向，普施
　　　法界眾生。

十二、願將法界眾生所有一切苦難，悉皆與我一人
　　　代受。

6. I vow that as long as there is a single asura who has not accomplished Buddhahood, I too will not attain the right enlightenment.

7. I vow that as long as there is a single animal who has not accomplished Buddhahood, I too will not attain the right enlightenment.

8. I vow that as long as there is a single hungry ghost who has not accomplished Buddhahood, I too will not attain the right enlightenment.

9. I vow that as long as there is a single hell-dweller who has not accomplished Buddhahood, I too will not attain the right enlightenment.

10. I vow that as long as there is a single god, immortal, human, asura, air-bound or water-bound creature, animate creature or inanimate object, or a single dragon, beast, ghost, or spirit, and so forth, of the spiritual realm that has taken refuge with me and has not accomplished Buddhahood, I too will not attain the right enlightenment.

11. I vow to fully dedicate all blessings and bliss which I myself ought to receive and enjoy to all living beings of the Dharma Realm.

12. I vow to fully take upon myself all the sufferings and hardships of all the living beings in the Dharma Realm.

十三、願分靈無數，普入一切不信佛法眾生心，令
　　　其改惡向善，悔過自新，皈依三寶，究竟作
　　　佛。

十四、願一切眾生，見我面，乃至聞我名，悉發菩
　　　提心，速得成佛道。

十五、願恪遵佛制，實行日中一食。

十六、願覺諸有情，普攝群機。

十七、願此生即得五眼六通，飛行自在。

十八、願一切求願，必獲滿足。

結云：

　　　　眾生無邊誓願度
　　　　煩惱無盡誓願斷
　　　　法門無量誓願學
　　　　佛道無上誓願成

13. I vow to manifest innumerable bodies as a means to gain access into the minds of living beings throughout the universe who do not believe in the Buddhadharma, causing them to correct their faults and tend toward wholesomeness, repent of their errors and start anew, take refuge in the Triple Jewel, and ultimately accomplish Buddhahood.

14. I vow that all living beings who see my face or even hear my name will bring forth the Bodhi resolve and quickly accomplish Buddhahood.

15. I vow to respectfully observe the Buddha's instructions and cultivate the practice of eating only one meal per day.

16. I vow to enlighten all sentient beings, universally responding to the multitudes of differing potentials.

17. I vow to obtain the five eyes, the six spiritual powers, and the freedom of being able to fly in this very life.

18. I vow that all of my vows will certainly be fulfilled.

Conclusion:

I vow to save the innumerable living beings.
I vow to eradicate the inexhaustible afflictions.
I vow to study the illimitable Dharma-doors.
I vow to accomplish the unsurpassed Buddha Way.

宇宙白

此首「宇宙白」，乃一九七二年二月十五日宣公
上人所作。當時金山禪寺舉行誦念「六字大明咒
」法會，四眾弟子，二十四小時不停地虔誠持誦
，無有倦怠，以祈禱世界和平。待七天法會圓滿
之後，上人有感而作此首「宇宙白」。「宇宙白
」表示整個宇宙都清淨了，沒有染污了，都變成
光明潔白的了。但要宇宙沒有染污，必須勇猛精
進，從「流血汗，不休息」做起。

　　　冰天雪地
　　　無數條小蟲凍斃　　且蟄眠
　　　靜裏觀察　　動中審諦
　　　龍爭虎鬥常遊戲
　　　鬼哭神嚎幻化奇
　　　眞實義絶言　　不思議　　當進趨
　　　大小泯　　內外非
　　　微塵遍　　法界周
　　　團圝個圓融　　互相無礙

White Universe

The Venerable Master composed the poem "White Universe" on February 15, 1972, during a session for recitation of the Six-syllable Great Bright Mantra (Om mani padme hum) at Gold Mountain Dhyana Monastery. The fourfold assembly of disciples sincerely recited around the clock without fatigue, praying for world peace. Upon completion of the seven-day session, the Venerable Master was inspired to compose this poem. "White Universe" signifies that the entire universe has been purified, so that it is luminous and immaculately white. In order for the universe to be free from defilement, we must cultivate vigorously and begin by "sparing neither blood nor sweat, and never pausing to rest."

Ice in the sky, snow on the ground.
Numberless tiny bugs die in the cold
    or sleep in hibernation.
In the midst of stillness you should contemplate,
    and within movement you should investigate.
Dragons spar and tigers wrestle in continual playful sport;
Ghosts cry and spirits wail,
    their illusory transformations strange.
Ultimate truth transcends words;
Not thought about or talked about,
    you ought to advance with haste.
With great and small destroyed, with no inside or out,
It pervades every mote of dust
    and encompasses the Dharma Realm,

雙拳打破虛空蓋
一口吞盡剎海源
大慈悲普度
流血汗　不休息

Complete, whole, and perfectly fused,
    interpenetrating without obstruction.
With two clenched fists, shatter the covering of
    empty space.
In one mouthful, swallow the source of
    seas of Buddhalands.
With great compassion rescue all,
Sparing neither blood nor sweat, and never pause to rest!

迴向偈

願以此功德　莊嚴佛淨土
上報四重恩　下濟三途苦
若有見聞者　悉發菩提心
盡此一報身　同生極樂國

Verse of Transference

May the merit and virtue accrued from this work
Adorn the Buddhas' Pure Lands,
Repaying the four kinds of kindness above
And aiding those suffering in the paths below.
May those who see and hear of this
All bring forth the resolve for Bodhi
And, when this retribution body is over,
Be born together in the Land of Ultimate Bliss.

南無護法韋馱菩薩
Namo Dharma Protector Weitou Bodhisattva

DHARMA REALM BUDDHIST ASSOCIATION
BUDDHIST TEXT TRANSLATION SOCIETY
PUBLICATIONS

法界佛教總會
佛經翻譯委員會

Lectures by the Venerable Master Hsuan Hua
宣化上人法音宣流

Chinese/English Buddhist Books & Tapes
中/英文佛經叢書、錄音帶目錄

編　號	宣化上人經典淺釋 (中文佛書)	冊	版本	價格 US
1BSC001	大方廣佛華嚴經淺釋	23	平裝	$173.00
1BSC002	華嚴經・普賢菩薩行願品淺釋	1	平裝	$6.00
1BSC071	大方廣佛華嚴經疏序淺釋	1	平裝	$6.00
1BSC072	大方廣佛華嚴經疏淺釋	2	精裝	$25.00
1BSC101	大佛頂首楞嚴經淺釋	2	精裝	$30.00
1BSC102	楞嚴經・大勢至菩薩念佛圓通章淺釋	1	平裝	$5.00
1BSC103	楞嚴經・五十陰魔淺釋	1	精裝	$20.00
1BSC105	楞嚴經・四種清淨明誨淺釋	1	平裝	$4.00
1BSC152	妙法蓮華經淺釋	2	精裝	$30.00
1BSC153	法華經・安樂行品淺釋	1	精裝	$12.00
1BSC155	法華經・觀世音菩薩普門品淺釋	1	平裝	$6.00
1BSC201	佛説四十二章經淺釋	1	精裝	$12.00
1BSC203	金剛般若波羅蜜經淺釋	1	精裝	$10.00
1BSC204	金剛般若波羅蜜經淺釋	1	平裝	$7.00
1BSC205	般若波羅蜜多心經非台頌解	1	平裝	$5.00
1BSC206	藥師琉璃光如來本願功德經淺釋	1	精裝	$12.00
1BSC208	佛説阿彌陀經淺釋	1	精裝	$10.00
1BSC211	地藏菩薩本願經淺釋	1	精裝	$20.00
1BSC212	大悲心陀羅尼經淺釋	1	精裝	$20.00
1BSC214	六祖法寶壇經淺釋 (革新版)	2	精裝	$30.00
1BSC215	六祖法寶壇經淺釋	1	平裝	$8.00
1BSC216	永嘉大師證道歌淺釋	1	平裝	$6.00
1BSC217	永嘉大師證道歌詮釋 (附圖)	1	平裝	$6.00
1BSC218	勸發菩提心文淺釋 (1985 年)	1	平裝	$7.00
1BSC901	大乘百法明門論淺釋	1	平裝	$6.00
1BVC002	佛遺教經淺釋	1	平裝	$8.00

編號	宣化上人開示 (中文佛書)	冊	版本	價格 US
1BKC003-4	宣化上人開示錄 (五冊合訂)	2	精裝	$35.00
1BKC007-12	宣化上人開示錄	6	平裝	@$6.00
1BKC013	宣化上人開示錄 (一九九三年訪臺開示)	1	平裝	$7.50
1BKC014	人生要義	1	平裝	$6.00
1BKC015	佛教新紀元 (訪歐開示)	1	平裝	$7.00
1BKC017	春日蓮華	1	平裝	$8.00
1BKC018	宣化上人法語開示	1	平裝	$6.00
1BKC019	教育救國	1	平裝	$8.00
1BKC020	道德救國	1	平裝	$8.00
1BKC030	照妖鏡 (宣化上人經典開示選輯 1)	1	平裝	$7.00
1BKC031	菩提本無樹 (宣化上人經典開示選輯 2)	1	平裝	$7.00
1BKC032	地獄不空 (宣化上人經典開示選輯 3)	1	平裝	$10.00
1BKC033	千手千眼 (宣化上人經典開示選輯 4)	1	平裝	$10.00
1BKC034	上宣下化老和尚偈讚歌詠專輯 (彩色盒裝)	1	精裝	$100.00
1BKC040	世紀末鐘聲 (宣化上人語錄 1)	1	平裝	$5.00
1BKC058	十法界不離一念心	1	平裝	$6.00
1BKC059	法界唯心	1	平裝	$7.00
1BKC060-1	水鏡回天錄 (正文)	2	精裝	$20.00
1BKC062	水鏡回天錄白話解 (帝王篇)	1	平裝	$10.00
1BKJ001	春日蓮華 (日文版)	1	平裝	$5.00
1BKJ002	十法界不離一念心 (日文版)	1	平裝	$5.00

事蹟傳記

1BBC001	再增訂佛祖道影	4	線裝	$25.00
1BBC003	宣化上人事蹟	1	平裝	$10.00
1BBC004	上宣下化老和尚略傳	1	平裝	$6.00
BB002	虛雲老和尚年譜	1	平裝	$6.00

編　號	其他中文佛書	冊	版本	價格 US
2BSC001	大方廣佛華嚴經 (經文/漢語拼音)	12	精裝	$100.00
2BSC002	大方廣佛華嚴經 (經文/注音/盒裝)	6	袖珍	$25.00
2BSC101	大佛頂首楞嚴經 (經文/注音)	1	袖珍	$10.00
2BSC102	大佛頂首楞嚴經 (經文)	2	線裝	$30.00
2BSC103	大佛頂首楞嚴經 (經文/漢語拼音/大本)	1	精裝	$20.00
2BSC104	大佛頂首楞嚴經 (經文/漢語拼音/中本)	1	精裝	$15.00
2BSC140	楞嚴咒 (護照本)	1	平裝	$4.00
2BSC141	楞嚴咒‧大悲咒‧十小咒 (袖珍本)	1	平裝	結緣品
2BSC151	妙法蓮華經 (經文/漢語拼音/大本)	1	精裝	$20.00
2BSC152	妙法蓮華經 (經文/漢語拼音/中本)	1	精裝	$15.00
2BSC202	地藏經 (經文/漢語拼音)	1	精裝	$10.00
2BSC204	法滅盡經 (經文)	1	平裝	$2.00
2BSC205	誌公禪師因果經 (經文)	1	精裝	$12.00
2BSC207	普賢菩薩行願品等六經咒 (經文)	1	平裝	$6.00
2BSC209	楞伽經註	2	平裝	$12.00
2BSC210	楞伽經會譯	4	平裝	$24.00
2BSC211	觀楞伽阿跋多羅寶經記	6	平裝	$36.00
2BVC002	梵網經菩薩戒本持犯集證類編	1	平裝	$3.00
2BVC003	優婆塞戒經講錄	1	平裝	$6.00
2BVC004	學佛行儀、五戒表解合訂本	1	平裝	$4.00
2BKC001	禪海十珍	1	平裝	$5.00
2BKC002	參禪要旨 (虛雲老和尚開示)	1	平裝	$5.00
2BKC005-6	佛教精進者的日記	2	平裝	$16.00
2BKC008	修行者的消息	1	平裝	$8.00
2BYC001	人之根 (注音版)	1	平裝	$7.00

編號 Code No.	中英雙語佛書 Bilingual Chinese/English Buddhist Books	冊 No. of Vols	版本 Edition	價格 Price US
1BSB071	大方廣佛華嚴經疏序淺釋 Flower Adornment (Avatamsaka) Sutra Preface	1	平裝 softcover	$5.00
1BSB101	楞嚴經五十陰魔淺釋 The Shurangama Sutra: The Fifty Skandha-Demon States	1	精裝 hardcover	$25.00
1BSB201	佛說四十二章經淺釋 The Sutra in Forty-two Sections Spoken by the Buddha	1	精裝 hardcover	$12.00
1BKB001-7	宣化上人開示錄 Ven. Master Hua's Talks on Dharma, Vol. 1-9	9	平裝 softcover	@$7.50
1BKB013	宣化上人開示錄（一九九三年訪臺開示） Ven. Master Hua's Talks on Dharma during the 1993 Trip to Taiwan	1	平裝 softcover	$10.00
1BKB014	十法界不離一念心 The Ten Dharma Realms Are Not Beyond A Single Thought	1	平裝 softcover	$7.50
1BKB015	正法的代表（袖珍本） A Sure Sign of the Proper Dharma	1	平裝 softcover	$3.00
1BKB016	百年大事渾如夢（袖珍本） The Great Events of One Hundred Years Are Hazy As If a Dream	1	平裝 softcover	$3.00
1BKB017	皈依的真義（袖珍本） The True Meaning of Taking Refuge	1	平裝 softcover	$3.00
1BKB018	訪歐開示 Dharma Talks in Europe	1	平裝 softcover	$8.00
1BKB019	達摩祖師西來意（注音附圖/老少咸宜） The Intention of Patriarch Bodhidharma's Coming from the West (Appropriate for children and adults. Generously illustrated with black and white Chinese brush drawings.)	1	平裝 softcover	$15.00
1BBB001	虛雲老和尚畫傳集 Pictorial Biography of the Ven. Master Hsu Yun	1	精裝 hardcover	$15.00
1BBB002	虛雲老和尚畫傳集 Pictorial Biography of the Ven. Master Hsu Yun	2	平裝 softcover	@$8.00
1BBB003	宣化老和尚追思紀念專集（一） In Memory of the Ven. Master Hua's, Vol. 1	1	精裝 hardcover	$25.00
1BBB004	宣化老和尚追思紀念專集（二） In Memory of the Ven. Master Hua's, Vol. 2	1	精裝 hardcover	$35.00

編號 Code No.	中英雙語佛書 Bilingual Chinese/English Buddhist Books	冊 No. of Vols	版本 Edition	價格 Price US
1BBB005	宣化老和尚示寂週年暨 萬佛聖城成立廿週年紀念專集 In Memory of the First Anniversary of the Nirvana of Ven. Master Hsuan Hua and the 20th Anniversary of the City of 10,000 Buddhas	1	精裝 hardcover	$30.00
1BBB006	萬佛聖城成立廿週年特刊 Celebrating the 20th Anniversary of the City of 10,000 Buddhas	2	平裝 softcover	$4.00
2BBB201	萬佛聖城日誦儀規 City of Ten Thousand Buddhas Recitation Handbook	1	平裝 softcover	$7.00
2BBB202	初一、十五佛前大供儀規 The Meal Offering Before the Buddhas for First and Fifteen of Lunar Month	1	平裝 softcover	$5.00
2BBB203	大悲懺本 Great Compassion Repentance	1	平裝 softcover	$4.00
2BBB204	華嚴經普賢行願品‧華嚴普賢行願懺儀‧ 華嚴經疏序 (合訂本) Flower Adornment Dharmas: Conduct and Vows of Universal Worthy, Flower Adornment Repentance, Flower Adornment Preface (a set)	1	精裝 hardcover	$12.00
2BVB001	梵網經講錄 The Buddha Speaks the Brahma Net Sutra	2	平裝 softcover	$20.00
2BSC001	大方廣佛華嚴經 (中文經文/漢語拼音) Amitabha Sutra (sutra text only, With Pinyin Romanization)	12	精裝 hardcover	$100.00
2BSC003	大佛頂首楞嚴經 (中文經文/漢語拼音/大本) Shurangama Sutra (sutra text only, With Pinyin Romanization)	1	精裝 hardcover	$20.00
2BSC004	大佛頂首楞嚴經 (中文經文/漢語拼音/中本) Shurangama Sutra (sutra text only, With Pinyin Romanization)	1	精裝 hardcover	$15.00
2BSC151	妙法蓮華經 (中文經文/漢語拼音/大本) The Wonderful Dharma Lotus Flower Sutra (sutra text only, With Pinyin Romanization)	1	精裝 hardcover	$20.00
2BSC152	妙法蓮華經 (中文經文/漢語拼音/中本) The Wonderful Dharma Lotus Flower Sutra (sutra text only, With Pinyin Romanization)	1	精裝 hardcover	$15.00

編號 Code No.	中英雙語佛書 Bilingual Chinese/English Buddhist Books	冊 No. of Vols	版本 Edition	價格 Price US
2BSC202	地藏經 (中文經文/漢語拼音) Sutra of the Past Vows of Earth Store Bodhisattva (sutra text only, With Pinyin Romanization)	1	精裝 hardcover	$10.00
2BYB001	大龜王 (兒童彩色佛書/注音) The Giant Turtle (Buddhist story for young readers)	1	平裝 softcover	$10.00

Code No.	Commentary on Buddhist Sutras by Ven. Master Hua's (English Buddhist Books)	Price US
1BSE201	Amitabha Sutra	$8.00
1BSE151-60	Dharma Flower (Lotus) Sutra (1 set, 10 books)	$79.50
1BSE161-6	The Wonderful Dharma Lotus Flower Sutra (Vol. 11~16)	@$10.00
1BSE001-22	Flower Adornment (Avatamsaka) Sutra (1 set, 22 books)	$174.50
1BSE071-4	Flower Adornment (Avatamsaka) Sutra Prologue (1set, 4 books)	$38.00
1BSE411	Heart Sutra & Verses Without a Stand	$7.50
1BSE521	Medicine Master Sutra (softcover)	$10.00
1BSE101-7	Shurangama Sutra (1 set, 7 books)	$59.50
1BSE108	Shurangama Sutra, Vol.8: The Fifty Skandha-Demon States	$20.00
1BSE109	Great Strength Bodhisattva's Perfect Penetration	$5.00
1BSE681	Shastra on the Door to Understanding the Hundred Dharmas	$6.50
1BSE682	Sixth Patriarch Sutra (hardcover)	$15.00
1BSE683	Sixth Patriarch Sutra (softcover)	$10.00
1BSE684	Sutra In Forty-two Sections	$5.00
1BSE685	Sutra of the Past Vows of Earth Store Bodhisattva (hardcover, commentary)	$16.00
1BSE687	Song of Enlightenment	$5.00
1BSE811	Vajra Prajna Paramita (Diamond) Sutra	$8.00
2BSE681	Sutra of the Past Vows of Earth Store Bodhisattva (softcover, sutra text only)	$5.00
1BBE451	Records of High Sanghas	$7.00

Code No.	Biographical (English Buddhist Books)	Price US
1BBE452	Records of the Life of the Ven. Master Hua, Vol. 1	$5.00
1BBE453	Records of the Life of the Ven. Master Hua, Vol. 2	$8.00

Ven. Master Hua's Talks on Dharma
(English Buddhist Books)

Code No.		Price US
1BKE031	Buddha Root Farm	$4.00
1BKE211	Herein Lies the Treasure Trove, Vol. 1	$6.50
1BKE212	Herein Lies the Treasure Trove, Vol. 2	$6.50
1BKE291	Listen to yourself, Think Everything Over, Vol. 1	$7.00
1BKE292	Listen to yourself, Think Everything Over, Vol. 2	$7.00
1BKE551	The Ten Dharma Realms Are Not Beyond a Single Thought	$4.00
1BKE641	Water Mirror Reflecting Heaven	$4.00

Other English Buddhist Books

Code No.		Price US
2BKE351	News from True Cultivators, Vol. 1	$6.00
2BKE352	News from True Cultivators, Vol. 2	$6.00
2BKE551	Three Steps, One Bow (一禮三千)	$5.00
2BKE6419	With One Heart Bowing to the City of 10,000 Buddhas (1 set, 9 books)	$63.00
2BKE650	World Peace Gathering	$5.00
2BYE061	Cherishing Life, Vol. 1	$5.00
2BYE062	Cherishing Life, Vol. 2	$5.00
2BYE151	Filiality:The Human Source, Vol. 1	$5.00
2BYE152	Filiality:The Human Source, Vol. 2	$5.00
2BYE211	Human Roots-Buddhist Stories for Young Readers, Vol. 1	$5.00
2BYE212	Human Roots-Buddhist Stories for Young Readers, Vol. 2	$5.00
2BME481	Songs for Awakening	$8.00

郵購須知

郵費及手續費:
每六片錄音帶照一本書計費。郵購不足六本書，照下列計費法：
郵購超過六本，請將郵購單寄至上列地址估計費用。

美國境內： 若購買一本書$2.00 美元。二本書以上每冊$0.75 美元。
以四級郵遞，需時兩星期至一個月。

美國境外： 若購買一本書$2.50 美元，二本書以上每冊$1.25 美元。
陸運。郵遞容易遺失之地，請掛號郵寄：
每包十本書另加郵資$3.75 美元。
郵件若有遺失，本會不負任何責任。郵遞時間需時二至三個月。

■加州居民另加上 8.25%之稅金。瑜伽區另加上 7.25%之稅金。
■支票抬頭請寫 D.R.B.A.
郵購請先付款，包括郵費及手續費。郵購單請寄：

> **佛經翻譯委員會** Buddhist Text Translation Society
> **萬佛聖城** Sagely City of Ten Thousand Buddhas
> 2001 Talmage Road, P.O. Box 217
> Talmage, CA 95481-0217 U.S.A.
> 電話: (707) 462-0939
> 傳真: (707) 462-0949

或

> **佛經翻譯委員會** Buddhist Text Translation Society
> **國際譯經學院** International Translation Institute
> 1777 Murchison Drive
> Burlingame, CA 94010-4504 U.S.A.
> 電話: (650) 692-5912
> 傳真: (650) 692-5056

錄音帶及書籍於法界佛教總會所屬道場，及有些書局，均可請得。

Ordering Information

Postage & Handling:
The following rates for postage and handling apply to orders of six or fewer books. Up to six audio tapes count as one book. On orders of more than six books, we suggest that purchasers submit their orders for a precise quote on postage and handling costs.

United States: $2.00 for the first book and $0.75 for each additional book. All publications are sent via special fourth class. Allow from two weeks to one month for delivery.

International: $2.50 for the first book and $1.50 for each additional book. All publications are sent via "book rate" or direct mail sack (surface). For countries in which parcels may be lost, we suggest orders be sent via registered mail for an additional $3.25 per parcel of ten books each. We are not responsible for parcels lost in the mail. Allow two to three months for delivery.

■ California residents add 8.25% tax. 7.25% tax for Ukiah area.
■ Make checks payable to: D.R.B.A.

All orders require prepayment, including postage and handling fees, before they will be shipped to the buyer. Submit order to:

Buddhist Text Translation Society
Sagely City of Ten Thousand Buddhas
P.O. Box 217, Talmage, CA 95481-0217 USA
Phone: (707) 462-0939; Fax: (707) 462-0949

or to:

Buddhist Text Translation Society
International Translation Institute
1777 Murchison Drive, Burlingame, CA 94010-4504 USA
Phone: (650) 692-5912; Fax: (650) 692-5056

Most branches of the Dharma Realm Buddhist Association, as well as some retail booksellers, also offer Buddhist Text Translation Society publications for sale.

法界佛教總會
Dharma Realm Buddhist Association Branches
Home Page: http:\\www.drba.org
Main Branch:
萬佛聖城
The City of Ten Thousand Buddhas
P.O. Box 217, Talmage, CA 95481-0217 U.S.A.
Tel: (707) 462-0939　Fax: (707) 462-0949

國際譯經學院 The International Translation Institute
1777 Murchison Drive, Burlingame, CA 94010-4504 U.S.A.
Tel: (650) 692-5912　Fax: (650) 692-5056

法界宗教研究院 (柏克萊寺)
Institute for World Religions (at Berkeley Buddhist Monastery)
2304 McKinley Avenue, Berkeley, CA 94703 U.S.A.
Tel: (510) 848-3440　Fax: (510) 548-4551

金山聖寺 Gold Mountain Monastery
800 Sacramento Street, San Francisco, CA 94108 U.S.A.
Tel: (415) 421-6117　Fax: (415) 788-6001

金聖寺 Gold Sage Monastery
11455 Clayton Road, San Jose, CA 95127 U.S.A.
Tel: (408) 923-7243　Fax: (408) 923-1064

法界聖城 The City of the Dharma Realm
1029 West Capitol Avenue, West Sacramento, CA 95691 U.S.A.
Tel/Fax: (916) 374-8268

金輪聖寺 Gold Wheel Monastery
235 North Avenue 58, Los Angeles, CA 90042 U.S.A.
Tel/Fax: (323) 258-6668

長堤聖寺 Long Beach Monastery
3361 East Ocean Boulevard, Long Beach, CA 90803 U.S.A.
Tel/Fax: (562) 438-8902

福祿壽聖寺 Blessings, Prosperity, and Longevity Monastery
4140 Long Beach Boulevard, Long Beach, CA 90807 U.S.A.
Tel/Fax: (562) 595-4966

華嚴精舍 Avatamsaka Hermitage
11721 Beall Mountain Road, Potomac, MD 20854-1128 U.S.A.
Tel/Fax: (301) 299-3693

金峰聖寺 Gold Summit Monastery
233 First Avenue West, Seattle, WA 98119 U.S.A.
Tel/Fax: (206) 217-9320

金佛聖寺 Gold Buddha Monastery
248 E. 11th Avenue, Vancouver, B.C. V5T 2C3 Canada
Tel/Fax: (604) 709-0248

華嚴聖寺 Avatamsaka Monastery
1009 Fourth Avenue S.W., Calgary, AB T2P 0K8 Canada
Tel/Fax: (403) 234-0644

法界佛教總會駐華辦事處（法界佛教印經會）
Dharma Realm Buddhist Books Distribution Society
臺灣省臺北市忠孝東路六段 85 號 11 樓
Tel: (02) 2786-3022, 2786-2474　Fax: (02) 2786-2674

紫雲洞觀音寺 Tze Yun Tung Temple
Batu 5 1/2, Jalan Sungai Besi, Salak Selatan, 57100 Kuala Lumpur, Malaysia
Tel: (03)782-6560　Fax:(03) 780-1272

佛教講堂 Buddhist Lecture Hall
香港跑馬地黃泥涌道 31 號 11 樓
31 Wong Nei Chong Road, Top Floor, Happy Valley, Hong Kong, China

宣化上人開示錄（八）

西曆二〇〇一年一月二日・中英版平裝
佛曆三〇二七年十二月八日・釋迦牟尼佛成道日・初版

發行人　法界佛教總會
出　版　法界佛教總會・佛經翻譯委員會・法界佛教大學
地　址　Dharma Realm Buddhist Association &
　　　　The City of Ten Thousand Buddhas
　　　　2001 Talmage Road, Talmage, CA 95481-0217 U.S.A.
　　　　電話: (707) 462-0939　傳真: (707) 462-0949

　　　　The International Translation Institute
　　　　1777 Murchison Drive Burlingame, CA 94010-4504 U.S.A.
　　　　電話: (650) 692-5912　傳真: (650) 692-5056

倡　印　萬佛聖城
　　　　The City of Ten Thousand Buddhas
　　　　2001 Talmage Road, Talmage, CA 95481-0217 U.S.A.
　　　　電話: (707) 462-0939　傳真: (707) 462-0949

ISBN 0-88139-855-1

● 佛典所在，即佛所在，請恭敬尊重，廣為流通。